Book One of the *My Life With Angels* Series

Rebel Writer

Rebel Writer

Secrets of The Extraordinary Life Hidden in the Page

By

Lee Travathan

ISBN 1-58500-397-2

About the Book

Rebel Writer, Secrets of The Extraordinary Life Hidden in the Page, is one of the most outstanding, unique, and fascinating books available to writers, and those who long to write, today. It is thought provoking, funny, profound and magical, say her preview readers.

"Lee Travathan's secret life with the page will hold you spell bound. I could not put it down!" says a man in his early seventies, who has never written, and began writing deep and profoundly from the page after reading the first chapter.

"I was salivating! I want more!" says a television producer.

"I love the way she writes. I got so excited reading my sample chapters that I can barely wait to read the rest of the book." says another preview reader. "She has a way to say things that blows me away. I think to myself, she's done it, she's found the words I couldn't find."

This book is for those who write regularly, those who have never written, and those who have dreamed of writing. Lee Travathan has a special relationship with the page that allows her to write in a manner uncommon.

She shows you how to do the same.

Her methods have helped others to release writer's block and uncover their own secret life with the page. Her style is one of a kind: sassy, whole, gripping and spiritual, say her readers.

Her methods and theories are revolutionary by most standards. And her following is growing rapidly, especially within the Hollywood film community, where she lives and conducts workshops on Rebel Writing.

"Lee Travathan is a unique woman having a passionate love affair with the page. She and the page talk and I love to read what they talk about!" says another preview reader.

Lee Newman, musician and actor, great grandson of Eddie Cantor and Jimmy Mchugh, says, "She's sharp, funny, bright, personal and sexy. Her outgoing personality grabs you and the aura around her makes one glad to know her. I love the things she has to say on and off the page. She radiates life! She is a Rebel Writer."

"Read it and weep... or laugh at my rebel life with the page." says Travathan. "Just read the book. I wrote it for you. You have things to say that you're not saying. Listen to the page... It has secrets to tell you about yourself and that's the best reason, and the most important reason, to read this book. You are worth uncovering those secrets for."

Life is happening
inside the page.

Lee Travathan

Dedication

To that which is all that we are.
To that which loves unceasingly and irreverently.
To that which is incomparable.
And to that which is completely misunderstood living in the page and in us.
Thanks Big Sweetie, for your unconditional, unabashed, and fiercely determined commitment to me.

In quiet times, late at night, I think about how lucky I am to have the life I have. Tears break loose from the dam within, streaming down my face, ancient and warm and comforting. And in those moments… those unspeakably precious moments, I kiss the cheek of God and am kissed.

As I sail off to sleep, a whisper of words affirm, "Ah, my love, you have done a very good thing today." I grin and recede into the fluid darkness surrounded by a light that no other can see, caressed by a lover known to so few. And I think to myself… life is good to me.

It was not always that way, and I can never forget how far I've come to meet today. Nor can I forget the angels of the seen and unseen, that blew vigorously and long their mighty breaths into my soul, that I could soar with eagles and retrieve the dreams once lost or broken. They saw a light in me because they are lights, and their love became the blood that kept my heart pumping courage into my actions. To these angels, I owe my very life.

To Papa Lou and Dorothy Pauletto, my adopted parents, I offer wings and trumpets. As well as this worn but good heart so ancient. Without them, I would have never known what it is like to have real parents that love unconditionally and assertively. You are my deepest dream come true.

To my adopted sister, Lady Di Harshman, how will I ever put into words the miracle you have been in my life these past fifteen years? You were born with wings, towing along the promise of finding me just when I needed to love you. And I do love you so with all my heart, Sis… with God as my witness, for all time and forever, I commit to that love.

For my children, Patrick Charles and Kathaleen, you are the best show in town and I would not have missed you for anything. Thank you for choosing me, for splendid moments that I will treasure far into other lifetimes, and for thinking me to be undeniably "cool." Kate, I especially thank you for staying when the angels called. I'd fight those unfaithful doctors for you all over again if I had to. You are amazing.

There are numerous friends not mentioned here whom I have thanked personally off the page. Still, I must mention actress, Sally Kirkland, author, David Brin, hockey great, Wayne Gretzky, and filmmaker, Robert Rodriguez, for being unintentional angels well used by Creation's hand for inspiration, friendship, instruction, or simple comfort. Many deserved thanks to you. Special thanks to young writers Lindsay Spann, Jennifer Clark, and Neil Lee Thompsett… the ones who go for it. I absolutely love your spirit!

And to the angel of Sanctuary, thanks for unbreakable and relentless belief and encouragement… you know my heart.

Bob, this one's for you.

This book is for those who have gone to the page and who have not yet. All individuals are rebel writers… even if you are a secret unto yourself, and to the world.

Lee Travathan

Contents

Disclaimer

This book is designed to provide one writer's views and opinions regarding the intricacies of her life and the lives of others, used for the purpose of example, to educate the reader in the true art of rebel writing. Although the material is based upon factual aspects of Ms. Travathan's life in and outside of Hollywood, some names, situations, and events have been altered or fictionalized for the sake of privacy for all parties concerned. The point of the example has been maintained within this process. When an issue need be unaltered for the sake of the writer's personal integrity, for the advancement of mankind, or to preserve constitutional rights, it has been left alone.

The writing examples from other writers have not been altered and are deeply and greatly appreciated.

This book is intended to complement, amplify, and supplement other text written about writing and to provoke spiritual thinking on and off the page. Those who use this text should consider it an artistic work of the writer bearing her thoughts, opinions, and ideas. It is not intended to reflect the views of others unless indicated.

The sole purpose of this text is to educate and entertain. The author or publisher shall have neither liability nor responsibility to any person or entity with respect to any loss or damage caused or alleged to be caused directly or indirectly by the information contained in this book.

It is accurate only up to the printing date. Any questions, thoughts, and comments from readers may be directed to the writer.

All attempts have been made to catch mistakes, in content or typographical, and all attempts were made to clear permissions where knowingly required. If there has been an error, the writer apologizes and a correction will be made in subsequent editions.

If you do not wish to be bound by the above, you may return this book for a full refund.

Author's Note

'Who are you?' said the Caterpillar.

This was not an encouraging opening for a conversation. Alice replied shyly, 'I – I hardly know, sir, just at present – at least I know who I was when I got up this morning, but I think I must have been changed several times since then.'

Lewis Carroll, Alice's Adventures in Wonderland

Lewis Carroll mastered words. In *Through the Looking Glass*, Alice asks Humpty Dumpty whether you can make words mean different things. 'The question is,' said Humpty Dumpty, 'which is to be master – that's all.'

'That's a great deal to make a word mean,' Alice said in a thoughtful tone.

'When I make a word do a lot of work like that,' said Humpty Dumpty, 'I always pay it extra.'

Lewis Carroll is one of my favorite writers. He was a rebel writer who wrote artfully from his soul and deep *from* the page. He and I share an uncommon understanding – the page is waiting for you to show up. It has things to tell you. You need not tell it what to say for it is waiting to tell you about the mysteries hidden in its vast and magnificent world.

Words are your servants and they are eager to be at your charge. Thank them for their efforts and they will share their inner world with you relentlessly. You will find that it is your world too. The page can be your best friend in good times and bad. You and the page are a precise marriage. You were born to meet, court, and wed.

The page is outrageous. It is extreme. Completely uncompromising. It bids that I visit and visit often. I admit to a weakness in this area of my life… I absolutely *cannot* resist that call.

Dates have been cancelled, lovers who complained have been left to fend for themselves, and days have been lost to my passion in the page. It is not unusual for a special man in my life to awaken to an empty spot late at night where I have been.

A wise man knows that the page and I are entranced in the grips of bracing seduction. A character is about to be born for an upcoming movie… or my mother who passed has something to say that she could not say before her death… or a problem that I've been mulling over has met its answer. A wise man knows how to handle my extravagant unleashed passions. A few determined and well-executed kisses can lure me back to bed.

The page will always be there for me to return to; the man may not be.

There are few things in life that I am more passionate about than the page. My God and my children, grandchild, adopted family, and my love of country are the only solid parallels. Someday a man will fit into the line-up and my passions will expand to meet him.

Writing is a magically sensual and spiritual act for me. It is my best friend, my wisest council, and my greatest lover – thank goodness, because it is sheer suppression to be without one. A sacred lover with strong spiritual values, human or otherwise, is an unmatchable gift. The page and I constitute a romantic relationship of the truest kind, an unconditional love between the magic and myself. It is pure ecstasy.

Love, at its heights, is an art form. A blessed opportunity to live an extraordinary life. The most uncompromising lovers save each other from an empty and unspeakable doom of moments missing magnificent synergy, a passionate sort of interdependence of natures. Real love, honest love, gives of itself fully to its lovers. Imaginary cosmic lines of limitation are crossed. The page gives of itself to me… mysteries and all. Limitation fades into the nothingness from which it came and a new life takes over.

Here I connect with that which created me from the deepest love possible. Over and over, my spiritual lover takes me home to peace and comfort, even in the midst of this world's cynical madness. Life is extremely secured here, safe and merciful.

Since I could put the pen to paper, words that write themselves *out* from the page on my behalf have been the most substantial aspects of my emotional and creative growth. I learned a long time ago that if you want to expand who and what you believe yourself to be, you must open your toolbox to new tools. Use what God gives you to build with, even if it makes no logical sense to do so. Be open to beauty that can't be seen with the common eye and you will know your own beauty in a way you never have before.

That's my story. I use what God gives me. I come to the page to talk with the parts of myself that like to hide from me. I also talk to God here, angels, Jesus, Mother Mary, or friends who have passed with words left unspoken. Everyone is listening for your words of welcome. I talk to pictures that harbor stories, as well as other objects, and I chatted with my children and my granddaughter before birth, just so they would feel welcomed when they arrived into the harsh environment of the delivery room. Everyday I ask the page what is important to know. It always tells me.

In short, I talk to whoever I want, whenever I want, wherever I want, and for whatever reasons I decide are important. And you can do the same. The page has no limitations… people do. You can change that in your life.

I did not first come to the page by accident. I don't believe in accidents. I came because it was part of my plan in being here on earth. We all have a plan and it is absolute pure perfection, no matter what our egos say in moments of brutish brat chatter.

In this book you will read about a little girl much like Alice in Wonderland. She fell to earth and landed in a hole filled with mysteries, had an outlandish adventure, and, yes, she almost got her head chopped off, too. But she became bigger than her smallest self, sometimes smaller, and she found out who she was. She had help along the way, angels of an odd sort, but angels all the same. They directed her and helped her make brave choices.

I do not remember a time in my life when I did not know about the angels who abide me. They've never left my side. Late one freezing winter Missouri night during my ninth year, I woke up from a heavy sleep to a very awkward feeling. I sensed energy around me that I thought might be God, except he was not like the vengeful and arrogant God I heard about often. The energy was kind, more like the guy next door or my best friend than one who came to condemn me.

An overwhelming nudge compelled me to bolt from the bed and follow instructions. I had no idea what was actually going to happen. After fumbling around in the dark, I found notebook paper, a pencil, and a flashlight. I sat on the cold linoleum floor in a drafty corner of the back porch kitchen and began to put down whatever I sensed brewing inside me. I just let my hand move to the words.

God showed up as a temperate and sympathetic awareness. He introduced me to the angels I already felt hanging around and we all started talking on the page that night. A miracle had happened to a little girl who dared to ask, "What's the truth about God?" The communication then was as it is today, wise, safe and healing.

I wrote this book because I have something vital to say and because you have something equally as important to say. I did not write alone. You should know that. When you go to the page, you will never be alone there.

Today I know that the page will help me know what I need to know and see what I need to see. As a writer and filmmaker living and working in Hollywood, I count on the mysteries in the page to help me write books and scripts. I don't have to *put* the words on paper or design the characters for my independent films… these elements are waiting inside the page to be made known. My job is to give them breath, to write them *out*. I am to deliver them into the world by my own hand.

The page has proven to me that most of what I learned about life growing up was incorrect. That's not a good or bad thing, it's just that there is another way. There are many other ways to the same place. We are all trying to get there in one way or another. That's what I came to the page to show you, another way that you can use for life.

We have gravely underestimated our personal worth and value to the whole of the world. Within us lives a roaring bravery that is rarely accessed. We look outside ourselves for life altering answers when *we* are the truth. The world is filled with fear-filled lies and foolery, as well as beauty. The beauty is missed if sought with the eyes of fear. But the page has no fear and it has no flaws. It sees you evenly. You are more beautiful and multifaceted than you might know. You *are* actually made in the creator's image… those are not just words. You've been endowed with infinite possibilities and probabilities. We are all more loved than most can imagine or accept and we have not owned this present. The page has owned it. It can help you to do the same.

You have things to say that you are not saying to yourself or others. I'd bet on it. But you may be afraid of the writing process because you've been taught a lot of mythology about it. I'm here to explode that mythology.

Your teachers did not teach you what all the great ones knew. Life is happening in the page. It is there to be discovered, like your heart and soul are here to be discovered. So that's the big secret in life… we are not here to create, we are here to discover what has already been created. We are children exploring a vast universe of miracles seemingly for the first time. Writing can help us do that. I explode the myths around the process of writing so you can find comfort with the page where love awaits. The lover in the page is another part of you that you may not have met yet. The time has arrived to meet the council, the best friend, and the lover in the page.

Inside of you is a rebel writer. Come with me and we will set it free!

Life is the amazing mystery occurring within you. When you speak of your lives, you speak of things that are happening to you out there in the world. It is rare that you dive into the deep waters to retrieve the pearls that can bring the mysteries of the universe alive. That is what can make your life rich...living the mysteries, letting them sink deep into your soul. Tasting them. Touching them. You can feel the hot lava of God's love pulsating through your veins. Hear us and you will hear your own deepest wisdom. You know more than you profess. Take the risk to be different in your world and you will kiss the face of God.

We watch you skirt the shallow waters where it is safe and dissatisfying. And we wish you knew what you are missing. You are missing the most basic elements, the true grit of the experience you came here to have. We use every avenue available to grasp your attention and hold it long enough to get the messages we convey. Wake up! Be alive! Live the mysteries! In the most ordinary of things, they exist.

Long ago an innocent and ancient child prayed at the bedside these words: God let me be an instrument of your peace upon the earth. Show yourself to me; let me see your face. She bid us welcome into her heart and we arrived. And now we bid you welcome into the magical world that surrounds her every move. Pull up a seat. The journey is about to begin! How do you start? Turn the page, and then the next, and then the next, until you find the treasures that are hidden therein.

Taken from The Angel Pages

Rebel Spirit

These unknown forces work deep within us, with the aid of the elements of daily life, its scenes and passions, and, when they burden us and oblige us to conquer the kind of somnolence in which we indulge ourselves like invalids who try to prolong dream and dread resuming contact with reality, in short when the work that makes itself in us and in spite of us demands to be born, we can believe that this work comes to us from beyond and is offered us by the gods.

From "The Process of Inspiration" by Jean Cocteau, translated by Brewster Ghiselin from Le Foyer des Artistes.

All my life I have believed that magic exists on an empty page. There is an unknown universe waiting here. Within the page rests opportunities for communication that is mystical, while being sensible, and extraordinary, while being utterly necessary. It is not the kind of communication that you have with your neighbor, your friends at work, or your lover. No, this route of communication is much more miraculous than that.

The page and its communications are what you have secretly and unconsciously craved all your life. It is what you have missed and mourned since you bombed in here from some unknown place where you existed prior to this birth. The mysteries of the page come from deep and vast seas of passion and never-ending changeless love. It is the sound and stable love that we each seek every day through other sources, never finding exactly what we are looking for.

The page is where we can go to break free from the ordinary, the expected norm of predictability in a mediocre world. And yet, the page is dependable, while being unpredictable in expression. This is where we encounter the Extraordinary Self that we came here to be. All the while the page is common, as common as the sun in the sky, Popsicles on a hot summer day, and our international sport, making love. This is the enchantment of the page. It is awesome and simple all at the same time, like you are.

The page knows you in a way that only God can know you. It understands your creative spirit. It knows your innocence and your thunder. It honors them both. It is here to serve you, to love you, and to bring you back to the God-like ownership of self that is one of your birthrights. It holds keys that unlock the deepest secrets of your heart, mind, and soul.

This is where the unexpected lives, that part of you that you try to hide even from yourself, but desperately want to know. This is where you go to meet the extraordinary true self that you are under all the layers of lies you have been told since your first breath.

You've always known that there is something more that you are not being told. And that there is something more that you are not telling yourself. You've secretly known your magnificence and you have craved the living of it. But a mousy little gnarly voice said, "Don't brag," and you listened, took your seat on the sidelines of life and watched everyone else play the game. You pretended you did not feel the explosive and beautiful energy inside roaring to get free. Perhaps you became numb to conceal the ache.

The feeling of numbness may appear as a vague sense of fragmented sadness, restlessness, or hopelessness, which seems to come from nowhere. Go to the page. Here, once forbidden truths are told in black and white, no longer to be ignored or set aside.

The page is home to the rebel spirit, the often-silent God-like deeper essence that you are. I know that essence so very well. The page has been my private rest stop; a place to retrieve hidden truths since that frigid Missouri night when my rebel writing days began as a burst of lightening blazing through my soul that left me transposed forever. In those moments I knew I was doing something different in this world, something special outside the predictable ordinary.

The world outside me did not change quickly, but I had instantly changed. Walls of mediocrity common to my internal environment crumbled and the door to an extraordinary world opened. Life's mysteries began to make sense. I began to see that there is a majestic plan for my life that is awe striking. I saw, as if in a vision, that your plan and mine are one in the same with a few details shifted here and there. But surely, we are in this thing together. The concept of separation is untrue and cruel and I rebel against it still today.

There is a rebel spirit in you, I just know it is there eager to be set free. I haven't met a single soul yet who did not have one.

This book is arranged in a casual style. This will help you write your extraordinary and commonly hidden life *out* from the page using examples that heal. Read the chapters one after the other first as presented or just open to the page that feels right. Contradictions are intended to allow our complex souls to find what they need on any given day.

Accepting yourself as a rebel writer changes you. You begin to say what you mean and mean what you say. That within itself is a miracle of the highest magnitude. Who you thought you were today may be incomparable tomorrow. You may get bigger, then smaller, smaller, and then bigger… but you will find your way out of the hole.

If you become numb like everyone else,
nothing changes.

Exercise: We all experience a quiet sense of numbness at times. It indicates a concealed or secret part of you attempting to break news to you. When that numb feeling hits, go to the page. It is faithfully awaiting your arrival.

Write these words: Part of me that is going numb, what are you trying to communicate?

Forget about grammar. Sit quietly and just listen. Write down everything you hear or sense and do not censor anything. If pictures flash through your mind, note them. They communicate as well. The answers do not need to make logical sense. Just listen and write. The part that is desperately attempting to get your attention has important information to deliver. It has been waiting for you to come to the page for so long, maybe for eons. When you are finished, read your page(s), but not before you feel complete.

Do the thing and you will have the power.
Ralph Waldo Emmerson

Personal Notes:

In Hollywood you hear a lot about writer's block, lack of inspiration, and disbelief in agents and producers.
You hear about how hard it is to think up an idea that a studio will buy, since they are buying mostly brainless ideas.
So writers sell their souls. They produce the junk the studios want and try to find a place for their pain.
It is a degrading time in this town for truly talented individuals.
I tell you this, and I am firm on my stand, you will meet a story that finds you appealing if you don't think about it, and if you make your own film and stop cutting your throat, you will meet your maker straight up.
Don't give me excuses; give me action.

Lee Travathan, speaking to a group of writers and filmmakers.

The Gift Was Left Unopened…

How much longer will you go on letting your energy sleep? How much longer are you going to stay oblivious of the immensity of yourself? Don't lose time in conflict; lose no time in doubt – Time can never be recovered and if you miss an opportunity it may take many lives before another comes your way again.

Bhagwan Shree Rajneesh

The first time I saw and touched a book I fell in love. It was a living thing with a beating heart, a long lost best friend that I could no longer live without, the seat of my yet unleashed passions. It spoke to me with the majestic voices of angels and I listened. It bid me entry into its vast and perfect world. The book knew where all the mysteries of the universe lived, it was written from that place.

It said, "*Touch me*. Be with me. I come from the known and the unknown, from the place of secrets, of cravings, longings, and desires. I am home to your heart."

I held the book gently and ran it across my face and then my arms, letting the essence of it sink rich and deep into my pores. I snuggled it up close to my heart and felt my body quiver like a leaf in the strong gale. I guided the spine and then the rest of its body over my lips and cheeks, feeling its angular perfect dimensions… so curious. I moved my hands over the worn cover slowly and deliberately, absorbing the tattered texture of old cloth and paper into my electric fingertips. It was the most beautiful thing I had ever seen. My body heaved with sobs of relief when the ancient scent of it got into my nose. Nothing existed but the book and myself.

Lost in the pages, I never wanted to be found. I have not since experienced an event so mystical, staggering, and spectacular as that perfect moment in time. It didn't matter that I could not read yet. It only mattered that I could touch the thing and hold it without it being taken away. I knew instantly that I would write books someday.

That mysterious day, and into the next, a frail, malnourished, terrified and breakable little girl; one who was so afraid to talk that she tugged on coattails and skirts to get a drink, asked for water, extra servings of her favorite foods, and her own special place at the table. It was the beginning of finding my voice.

Still, today, books turn me inside out in a way that nothing in the world has ever managed to neutralize. Even my favorite and most sensual lover of all time can not contrast my experience of *meeting the book.*

There is a brave soul out there in the sleepy sonnets of the yet unknown that can pull a tight second to the memory of such potent magic. Clearly, I sense his essence. I have yet to meet him and remain open.

I admit to being picky. Rugged, elegant, fine and spiritual men have a chance. A man without a spiritual heart has no chance at all. A man who is not afraid to get dirty while maintaining the ability to make a great suit look even better intrigues me. As with my books or movies, before I see them in front of me, I often get a glimpse of him sort of hanging out in the ethers.

You know the guy. He jumps off a sweaty horse, dusty and sloppy, suits up for dinner at a nice place, and makes your mouth water more than the food because he is just so incredibly tempting. And you know, without a doubt, that he is as delicious to kiss as he is to contemplate. He's characteristically sensitive.

When you sit back and quietly watch him he knows you're watching and he likes it, but he does not pretend for you. He knows himself too well to play unnecessary games; he's already got your attention. He's loaded with charm and charisma, but he does not abuse them. This man is playfully goofy and sensual while being clearly intelligent. Ah, such perfection! He exudes passion in the way he lives, is artistically creative, romantic, and a bit of a flirt. But his flirting is harmless. He sends up a skywriter to get your attention if he wants a bigger commitment from you. To just say it would be far too ordinary.

That's my guy.

Like my books and movies, he must bring the best of himself to my life. I can't take the time out for less than that.

There is a good chance he may wander along the same road as myself here in Hollywood. I tend to date actors, directors, writers and independent filmmakers like myself. I suspect he is either a writer or an actor, maybe both. He's hanging out with the rest of these guys somewhere around town at this very moment. They are the Hollywood wild bunch. Without them, this entire town would dry up to nothing but windswept streets and cloudy memories. Passion is their riveting trademark. This is their domain. They are the breaths palpitating through the air the rest of us inhale.

Yes, the man I want has to be grand to get my attention. He needs to mean something powerful within his own perception of Self. This man understands that power is how you perceive yourself. He knows what he's made of and he isn't afraid of it. I'm looking for the guy who can move my soul... a man of substance. Settling for less is just that, settling. You get what you ask for in one way or another. I've loved the rest, now I want the best. For the right guy, my books, written and yet unwritten, will make plenty of room.

I believe in a profound and comical creator, in true love, and in books and words. Books and the words in them have a major, often unspoken, design and intent. Even off the page words are the avenues that allow us to walk into each other's lives.

There is nothing more powerful to human beings than words. When Martin Luther King said, "I have a dream," your future changed, even if you were not born yet. The whole world began to spin from a different point of the compass.

When a battered woman says "No more!" to an abusive man then leaves the infected, feeble and diseased puppy behind; she strikes a stinging blow to the lives of abusive men she's never even met.

A woman endowed with Herculean faith is mighty. Mix that faith with impenetrable concrete and steel words, put them at her access and she can build a bridge that can change the lives of thousands of women all across the country, perhaps the world, if she is so determined. Never underestimate the power of a burning voice mixed with the power of the pen. Robbing a guy blind and leaving him for dead holds less power than a strong woman taking a pen to hand does.

Take a moment. If you are a woman who's been to this secret place of abuse where otherwise brave women hide, pick up a pen and start setting down a newsletter to help others who are still there. Check your resources, get a mailing list or get on the web, do what you must, and get to work! Be a beacon in the darkness, shine your light. Use your words to make a difference.

If you are a man recklessly living out this darkness, go now and get help. Know that you are worth it.

Every movement forward is a treasure to the whole. When a confident and reasonable man says "Yes!" to mature and nurturing love, daring to give a woman and himself the respect their love deserves, the dignity of women across the world begins to heal. We all unconsciously advance a step forward with a little more faith in each other.

When a *Rebel Writer* surfaces, discovers mysteries in the page and publishes, he or she risks everything known in the outside world to know the authentic inside story.

To the brave go the victories. The door opens for a million other previously silent rebels to walk through.

The mediocrity of the waking dead is dealt a nasty, startling, and forceful blow. Authenticity, the authenticity that is a forgotten birthright, is given breath and life and meaning. The species called *human* begins to make every precious moment count a little bit more outside the insidious cynical darkness of ordinariness to which we have become mutated. We begin to answer to a higher order of being. The phrase: *Know ye that ye are Gods,* becomes more real. We take our power back from the jaws of a quiet deadness far too common in our present lives.

In the end the rebel writer can not lose. None of us lose. All people, deep down, are rebel writers undiscovered. When one hits the mark we all gain a piece of another missing birthright, the ownership of the forbidden and hidden *Extraordinary Self*... the part of you attempting to get and hold your attention through any and every other means conceivable outside the page.

You may not want to publish what you write, but you need to be good enough to yourself to write the words anyway. They may be just what you wanted to acquire and what you were silently and blindly missing at a quiet but nagging level. Words have a life of their own and they are waiting to speak to you at any hour of the day or night. An enchanted life is sincerely happening inside the page, calling you to ownership. Your undiscovered life is here right now.

Anything you are ready to know can be known.

Do yourself a favor; don't wait to be ready. You were born ready to go deeper into the mysteries that are your life than you are right here in this very moment. Don't wait to have something perfect to write about. Grab something out of the air. Just do the thing. Write. How long you write does not matter, ten minutes here, and an hour there. Use what you find. Steal the time from the jaws of mediocrity.

Write what is in front of you. So the dog ate your best shoes, your child has a cold and you did not sleep last night, you're tired and hungry, there is never enough time, the house is a mess and the payment is late, again... whatever... just write! The pages that come may get you thinking about your life in a different way.

Suspend your judgements as you read this book. It is full of passion, courage, and rebel writing. Get hooked if you want, but do stop and write along the way. Forget grammar, spelling, and structure. I'm giving you permission. Just write what you think and feel and then go deeper into the thought and feeling, then deeper, then deeper. Keep going. We live in a holographic universe and it is not to be restrained. You can continue going deeper, excavating, for the rest of your life.

Don't censor what you write. Let the page *talk* to you. Trust that you hear it. Don't try to tell it what to say. *That's called writer's block.* You don't need it. *Writer's block is not common to the rebel writer's awareness or experience of life-giving extraordinary thinking.* I started listening and writing as a child with no understanding of these factors I've just mentioned. I was not following any pattern or known process. As the years passed, I continued to just write what I heard and I trusted it. Below is a cut of the words that were hidden in the page in my early teens during a particularly hard period of my life.

Today you may be tempted to say that you know me not. You do. What you remember of me in stolen moments will alter those moments within you.

Yes, these times are hard and seemingly unfair. When your heart hurts, come to me. I shall cradle your heart in my hands and rest your weary soul. Watch your world through my eyes and find the peace I offer. All that you see shall pass away. You are here to do great things that make your spirit soar. Others will fly with you and cast off from your belief in them. Let not these days before you slay you. Choose your master, master faith, and go into the darkness knowing I am there, too. You are never alone.

What a child can do, you can do.

My early pages were so mighty that I hid them under my mattress for the longest time, much like a young man hides his forbidden Playboy magazines. The words electrified me to the bone and the feeling of that intensity scared me.

At the time I had no physical *safe place*. I was brought up in a home filled with unpredictable rage that struck like lightning bolts. This created a thick and foreboding silence, blankness inside our walls. Had I shown anyone those stirring words from the page or a hint of my spine tingling joy, unmerciful and rabid punishment would surely have followed.

I grew up learning to lie about my feelings, even to myself. And I learned to keep the pages well hidden, to live with my secrets. I couldn't let anyone know that they existed. They were my only real happiness.

Happiness that went over a whisper was not allowed expression in our house. It was to be feared. An emotion might get stirred that woke someone up from his or her deep hypnosis. We simply could not have *that*. Hell broke into full fury when that happened. The eye of a hurricane was less dangerous than the emotional explosions in the house of lies.

Emotions were horribly disproportionate and inflammable within my birth family. The obvious lack of healthy emotions and discussions made me particularly nervous. I felt different than the rest of my family, disassociated and awkward, not included or accepted.

Having no physical resemblance only increased the feeling of confusion. I couldn't understand the way they lived, or learn to accept that I should simply follow suit without question. It was clear to me that a sickness, an uncontrolled disease, was lurking about in our house. Maybe everyone knew it was present. Still, we didn't talk about it. We didn't talk about anything. Whatever the cost the silence asked, we paid. I felt so horribly poor inside and saw no end to the cost of such emotional poverty.

The cost was towering, overwhelming, and escalating with each passing day. I learned that first hand the day my father beat me during the first summer I was discovering boys. I accepted an afternoon ride with a boy I knew from school who was older than I was. His parents had just given him a flashy new car for his birthday and we decided to take it for a spin around town. There were only two main streets, but we felt so incredibly cool and hip. We cruised the same streets over and over as we caught up on summer gossip, making sure everyone saw us. We did not just want to be cool; we wanted to be seen *being* cool. When a friend waved from the sidewalk we felt like giants! It was a precious time. He was a sweet boy with a crush on a pretty girl and the hottest car in town. This was his glory hour.

My father had a false expectation that I did the thing good girls were not supposed to do, and since preacher's daughters are, by some unspoken law, *good girls*, he set out in his car to find me. When he did, he ordered me home. Once there I was not given the chance to defend my innocence.

His rage was volcanic, scorching every inch of my skin. I imagined the shadow of death casting itself around me. The horrible thing I imagined happened when my father lost all control. He beat me relentlessly until he wore himself out. He then walked away without a word, leaving me a shattered mess as fragile as broken glass lying about on the living room floor. If

I could have drug myself away from that house that day I would have. With God as my witness, I wish I could have.

With each inch I moved toward the stairs leading to my attic bedroom, I became determined that if he ever pulled off his leather belt again or raised his hand to me, I'd fight back until one of us lay unconscious. Not me, I thought. Not me… I won't be the unconscious one. I schemed to run as far away as possible, change my name and find the emotional peace of mind I could then only dream about. That was my plan. And it was solid, like steel. Winning the fight was my only option.

Safety and peace were the fantasies that became my bed partners. I'd do anything to have them as reality.

Days passed slowly after that. Mostly in silence. I suspect my father knew where he stood with me. He could see it in my eyes; fire had replaced my child-like gentleness. He had become a dragon and I had become a dragon slayer, a true fighter and a determined survivor. No one was going to break me the way horses are broken. That's what I told myself.

I knew the truth hidden under the masks we wore; we could never go back to who we had been before the beating. We had become equal opponents on a new playing field. A silent war had been declared.

I rarely spoke to him after that betrayal. I was no longer a child and there was nothing more to say to the deaf-spirited man who was not listening in the house of lies. I was now fighting for my very soul and I was going to win. The fighter in me refused to let my spirit be broken. The page rose up to help me during private times. But for my father and I, the absence of real and meaningful conversation left a bottomless sinkhole, a pit of rage, between us. It resembled an open bleeding wound left unattended, bigger than the Grand Canyon and harder to cross.

I did not loose my virginity that summer to John, the boy from school, but I clearly lost my innocence to my father within a matter of fifteen minutes. I was brutally, severely, and unjustly violated. Then I was not allowed to speak of it. What my father did was more damaging than anything John wanted to do could have been.

The boy was trustworthy; I knew that when I got in the car. I was a smart girl, something my father always underestimated. He was a boy comfortable in his own skin with nothing to prove to me; he was a temporary safe place. My father had underestimated him as well. This boy respected me. I was not just another pretty girl, but someone much more special; an ugly duckling that he had watched turn into a long, graceful, beautiful swan right before his eyes. A long-time friend, an equal, a girl who made him laugh from an otherwise quiet place inside. I was the girl he could tell his secrets to.

On the other hand, my father was a man living in the desperate fear of being exposed as someone less than perfect, so afraid to look bad in the community. He did not respect himself, his flaws, or me. I began to see him as someone dangerous and I kept my distance.

He never touched me again.

Deadness came over the two of us like a dark thundercloud that never broke.

What you can't talk about you can't change for each other. My father and I developed an unspoken indifference within the deadness that became our new relationship. Any commitment I had to him as a daughter was broken, bluntly damaged and mostly lost. He never fought to heal the open cut that bled and oozed as he pretended not to notice. He never fought for my lost dignity; he never missed it the way I did.

I vowed that if I ever had children, I'd always fight for their well being. I vowed that my children would never feel the agony that I felt with my father. I would love them as if my very life depended upon it.

He never apologized for leaving my body and face black and blue, cut and welted. For the shame I felt over something I did not do. Or for the way the beating made me feel worthless and small… tragically and terminally ugly when I had just found my beauty. He never will apologize for these things.

Anything that mattered was swept under the rug at the good preacher's house. I stayed home for a couple of weeks faking a cold, cut off my long beautiful hair, and we all pretended that nothing sick or despicable ever happened in the house of lies.

The silence was unbearably loud, nearly deafening. My ears rang with resistance to it. I wanted to scream, but I knew no one would hear me. I was not sure that even I could hear myself anymore.

God handled my plight typically, by supplying me with the miracle of understanding and showing me that there were unusual advantages to being raised in an anesthetized house of deadened souls. I recognized that I wanted to make movies while I sat in my room healing. I had developed my natural acting ability and film eye over the years as a survival tool. With no true happiness to draw from, I made up scripts about happy, healthy, complex and interesting people unlike the ones I knew. They had to be alive somewhere, at the least, in the page. Universes existed in the page for me, surely people did, too.

Over and over, I visualized entire movies in my head, lots of them. My characters were fully alert and cared about each other intrinsically. They talked together, really had conversations, and had them about things that actually mattered aside from the weather. They did things together that were meaningful, not just for show. None of them were perfect and that was a grand thing. They danced and laughed; sometimes they cried together. Love was immediate and dependably present. They were not afraid of real emotions.

My characters showed love outwardly. I heard the words in my house on occasion but never saw the thing. Love was a mystery, except for the love that came from the page. That love kept me going.

Just off Main in a typical sleepy Missouri town no bigger than a postage stamp, life in the house of lies was a take it or leave it deal. My sister, Cynthia, and I woke up every morning to walk through invisible mine fields seeking safety and sanity that we were never to find. I desperately wanted a better life. Many times a day I prayed for it. And I knew that in some mysterious way, within one perfect moment, I'd be set free and I'd fly away forever. It is all that I lived for.

A beady-eyed and nearly insane little woman barely five feet tall ruled the roost. Bess bent my father's brain any way she wanted by running out in front of cars passing by the preacher's house, screaming not-so-crazy things about the events inside. If that didn't work, she found ways of embarrassing him in front of important church company. So, company stopped coming by. All company. Even my friends did not come around. They were all afraid of the mad woman. The crazier Bess became the more she gained complete control.

The only force more powerful than she was that vengeful God I heard about every day, the one that was going to get me if I messed up… I always messed up. He lived in the house of lies as well and held court there daily. He was the thunderous judge and jury, and to him, I had about as much value as the dust on the floor beneath my feet. No one ever won a case in his court of sins and sinners, especially not me. *Bad* little girls who took rides in cars with older boys who possessed penises went to a seriously evil place filled with eternal horrors from which you could never return. I was sure to end up there.

I rigorously refused to believe in this tyrannical God, which presented me another reason to go to hell. *This* deity was a mess! He needed major therapy. Maybe a lobotomy. And he was in control of the universe? That just never seemed right. I went to the page for comfort and found it.

In the page lived a good God, one that loved me and talked to me like a true friend. My God held no malice toward me; he did not want to see me suffer. From the page I received this message:

Watch the wind, dear love, for it is shifting. Freedom from suffering will come to one who demands it of me. Make me prove myself and I will. I gave you a voice that you will use to raise thunder across the universe, not that you would hide it in a well.

Do not live for the darkness. Live for the light. Become the light in the darkness and the darkness shall fade away into the nothingness from which it came. Be the love you seek unto yourself. Dear one, the winds change rapidly, blowing that which is old away when you are ready. Prepare the soil of your soul for a new harvest. Depend on my promises. Count on my love.

I didn't know what these words meant, but I was willing to find out. I started watching for signs of change. *My* God had never steered me wrong. I had to count on that consistency; I had nothing else to bank on.

Summers were the most dangerous times of the year. Little could be found to do in town except for an occasional street dance put on by the owner of the local newspaper. There was no movie theatre or sports center. No other planned activities to speak of. The kids in town and out in the country lived for the dances but, they were never enough. Too little, too late. Fourteen-year-old girls got pregnant and boys got drunk and killed themselves in auto accidents, or ended up in the Boonsville Correctional Facility.

My fourteenth summer was not unlike others outside the house, but inside, it was the most dangerous of all. It was then that my mentally ill stepmother heaved a knife to my chest at the kitchen sink while peeling potatoes for Sunday dinner. I happened by at the wrong time. My father reacted, pulled her off me, and threw her about fifteen feet into the next room where he demanded she stay. She landed like an iron anvil on the creaky old mahogany bed, screaming in sorrowful tones, "What are you doing to *me*?" as if I wronged her!

After years of begging my father to take some concise and defensive action before she killed my sister or me, he had awakened just in time to save my life.

I was shaken with the dynamics of the event. So, that's what it took to get his attention, I thought to myself. It had to be something so spectacular and extreme that the neighbors absolutely could not know about it. No police report, or ambulance, no messy truth exposed. No bodies lying around. No sins of my father uncovered. No atrocities to mar the good preacher's name.

When it was over, I nursed my wounds and silently called my father and I even. I did not have to say it, he knew. We all knew.

That day, just an hour after the attack, my sister and I served Sunday dinner as usual with my father at the head of the table. Bess stayed in her room and screamed in insane nonsensical babble patterns. We ignored her. Not a word was uttered. We never talked about it. Not ever. We all pretended that nothing happened.

The next summer my sister graduated from high school and the preacher delivered his usual commencement address outside in the dripping Missouri heat. Watching him there on the stage, he was a man I did not know and was not knowable to me. I watched my sister take her diploma and shake it into the air with a big smile… and in that moment I knew I never wanted that to be me - not in that place, not with that man on the stage.

I had been staying around to protect Cynthia from the wicked stepmother who had attempted to knock her face off with a cast iron skillet. And due to the fact that Bess told me she would smother us with our own pillows one night as we slept. I started locking us in each night. I believed she'd do it.

But the wind had indeed shifted. I refused to face another summer in the house of lies. My sister needed to get away and take care of herself. I told her that. These words were my graduation present: ***Please leave this terrible place.***

Later that night I took a small cheap suitcase, a spat of babysitting money, my precious pages, a prayer, a dream of writing books and making movies, and headed west to California.

My birth mother lived near Palm Springs. I didn't know her, but I needed to take a chance that she wanted to know me. She had said as much and I wanted to believe her. I knew so little about her that I had few expectations. I figured that if we did well together, I might actually have a *real* mother. That exciting thought inspired me to learn as much about her as I could.

What I soon found was as disturbing as what I left behind. She was not only a belittling and demeaning jealous sort of woman, but she did not want me. She didn't even like me. Guilt and shame became her trademark parenting tools. In the end, she said that I reminded her of all that she was not and she would have no part of that. My mother saw me as an exquisite child, tall and thin, graceful, ambitious and unusually talented, mentally gifted, charismatic… and beautiful, more beautiful than she had ever imagined being. It almost drove her mad. She and I were nothing alike; we were worlds apart.

Once I left her house I was disowned. If I saw her in town she walked right past me without even a glance my way. I thought I was going to die. I believed completely that my last chance for a family had died. One moment of seeing her cold and dispassionate eyes left me devastated for weeks.

No one wanted me… that was the bitter truth I had to learn to swallow and accept. I wasn't sure that anyone ever really had wanted me. I was a birth accident born of two people who did not love each other with too many children already. Sixteen years later, in the midst of my realization, I walked singularly in a strange world called California, no longer a child but not yet a woman. I was utterly alone and homeless with no one to turn to. So I held closely to all that I could call my own, maybe all that I had ever had… my pages, dreams, prayers, and kind angels.

Wanting more than the ordinary and uncertain life I knew cost me everything that I had ever known. The price I paid was undoubtedly excessive. But the freedom to be myself that I gained made it worth the costs.

A gift given to my birth family was left unopened, so I opened it myself. Inside I found an honestly beautiful young woman who meant something. Something mighty and consequential. She had the strength of a thousand armies and the faith of a small helpless child absent of all doubt. She was good and kind, filled with divine dignity. Every bone in her body was held together with creative marrow. She was a robust force holding value in this world. I loved her. I loved everything about her that my family could never see within the scope of their blindness. She and I were one, the priceless gift left unopened.

Whatever your experience in life, just go to the page. Be there. Be with you. Open the gift that you are. Unwrap it gently and kindly, a bit at a time if you need. If your life story is tragic like mine there are blessings hidden within the experience that the page can show you. Go to the page right now… it is awaiting your arrival.

Exercise: You've just read some things about my life that are disturbing. Certain details have been omitted to maintain privacy and some names have been changed for the same reason. This account is my experience and my experience only. It is not shared by my birth family still living in denial of these events. Rebel writers face such darkness to get to the other side where the light glows strong and bright, where life is dependable. The bigger picture affects the whole. You throw a pebble in your pool and I feel the ripples.

Pull out your pen and paper or go to the computer and answer these questions. Let it flow. Do this timed or untimed. If timed, do thirty minutes and stop. Go back later and repeat the exercise. See what has changed.

How do I feel about the writer's experience?

What thoughts or emotions did it invoke within me that speak of my life?

If my childhood was not tragic, what was it?

Pick one particular element of this chapter, *meeting the book*, the beating, leaving home, etc, and expand upon it. Become the little girl you just read about. How do you see her? Describe her.

Now describe the child you remember being. What do you like best about that child?

Write anywhere. Write everywhere.
Write everything.

To whom can I speak today?
I am heavy-laden with trouble
through lack of an intimate friend.

The Man Who Was Tired of Life
1990 BC

Deep Waters

Even to the creator himself, the earliest efforts may seem to involve commerce with disorder. For the creative order, which is an extension of life, is not an elaboration of the established, but a movement beyond the established or at the least reorganization of it and often of elements not included in it. The first need is therefore to transcend the old order. Before any new order can be defined, the absolute power of the established, the hold upon us of what we know and are, must be broken. New life comes always from outside our world, as we commonly conceive that world.

Brewster Ghiselin

In school we were taught to think and write safely and tactfully. That is all sweet and nice, but it won't help you navigate the deep end of the soul's ocean. The tempest becomes far too choppy to play life cautiously. The page is no place to be timid. You can't understand its plundering mysteries from a logical and safe position.

The real backbone of life is not logical. It is not candy-coated or articulate. It is everything in contrast to what we consider the norm. Real equals untidy. Untidy often equals exciting, cutting edge and radically important. Untidy often indicates a perfect creative order.

Our greatest inventors and heroes did not do well at following rigid rules and I don't either. That does not always set well with the timid of mind or weak of spirit… the secure love me and the insecure loathe me. I find it extremely difficult to eat life raw and maintain proper table manners. This means that I do make a mess as I sort out my life. Discovering the elusive secrets of your soul might… no, it will, mean breaking some ingrained spoon fed rules. Most of the time your writing won't be pretty or perfect.

Rebel writers write mostly from the backbone of life, the raw materials of *their* lives. They plunge into the deepest waters of the soul because they must; something indefinable drives them to proceed... like the way that salmon must swim upstream to spawn even if they die doing it. True rebel writing is not going to come out pretty. It is going to smear truth in your face and the faces of anyone who reads it. Thank God.

Let me give you an example. In my early twenties I helped teach a night course for writers in the San Francisco area. I went in as a student and was recruited by the professor after reading some of my rebel writing in class.

The group consisted of twenty some college students, two returning thirtysomethings and one older woman of seventy. Each week we wrote and read, then had coffee and cookies at the back of the room.

Two students other than myself drew everyone's attention each session when new material was read. One was the neat and ship-shape older woman and another was a young misfit unruly man who slouched in his seat and wore rumpled clothes. Full and perfect lips allowed him to flirt with all the girls even without words. One smile mesmerized and in one single second he had any young woman he wanted in his palm. His long wavy beach blonde hair (that I wished I had) flowed down to the center of his long back and framed his piercing midnight blue eyes. Heavily scuffed shoes with no socks or old worn sandals and shorts made for his winter attire. I adapted to a place in the middle. I was the struggling young mother of an infant son pretending to be in a satisfactory marriage with a brazen power hungry alcoholic, a California blue blood from a noted founding family. We all had things to say.

The older woman wrote lively and fascinating stories about her childhood in the Midwest. They were so alive that I could envision myself running through the meadows with her, my long calico skirt blowing in the wind, smelling fresh cut hay in the fields below. After she read everyone clapped. She smiled poetically and bowed courteously into her seat wearing a near purple face. This exact scenario played itself out each week.

I read about my connection to philosophical issues. My position was that of a social radical on the edge of action or disaster. I could go either way. For that matter, the whole world could have gone either way. I wrote about suppressed needs we all share that nobody likes to talk about, the heart of human mythology and the tragedy of our unclaimed genius. It was good material and I was honored by the response. Other students wanted copies of my work to read at home. I made them think.

The undisciplined and disorderly young man stood each week from his chair in a sort of matter of fact pose, and without the slightest effort, blew the socks off every person in that room! Where I made people contemplate, he made us feel so fiercely that boxes of tissues were passed, twice. All through break time noses were blown and trash cans filled.

To this day his words ring in my ears… *just hang it on the wall.* The piece spoke of his life in the perfect family, and the perfect prison. I see myself walking through the rooms of his exclusive family estate high on the hill overlooking San Francisco, noticing the prized family pictures hanging on the walls. Happy faces engaged in joyous events jump out at me from the sweeping gallery-like surfaces; faces that hide hideous and consuming pain, quiet personal and social suicides, unbearable secrets and fragile skeletons never exposed to the light. He has made me privy to this display through the power of his words.

Through his willingness to be exposed he touched into a core piece of every listener. We whispered across the long tables as he read, "Is he really saying that? Thank God, he's really saying that!" He said what we could not. We cherished every word. We hungered, no; we ached and starved for more. He was a rebel writer writing his backbone *out* of the page. It definitely was not pretty, but it moved the mountains between us. We became more real to each other.

Each week at the back of the room students told the older orderly woman how they enjoyed her entertaining pieces and then left her alone. What they did not tell her was that enough of goody two shoes is enough… they could not relate to her syrupy childhood. Why? It's simple. Nobody has a childhood like hers unless they are hiding something uncomfortable from themselves. Deep down we all knew that.

It was altogether just too pretty, never a muss or fuss, too perfect. Nothing out of place. You can only hear a few stories like that before you get bored silly. Whether listening to or reading a writer, we want a slice of them. We want a generous chunk of their heart, their soul, and their body. We want the truth of who and what they are or at least the truth of what they believe and feel strongly about, even if it hurts. We want *real*, not *reel* guts. This lady was willing to die with her secret self unexposed. She had never ventured out beyond the known outside the norm. She sure wasn't going to start down that road in our class. It would have been terrifying and death defying. No, she was clearly a take-no-risk and feel-no-pain kind of woman coloring inside the lines of life or painting by the numbers.

And Andy, our color out-of-the-lines rebel writer, what happened to him at the back of the room? Each student, except for the robotic and well-behaved lady, hung on his every word. They treated him like the prodigal son who came home. He was lavished with hugs and kisses. He received thank you cards and gifts. Students wrote about him in their pieces and called the campus newspaper to get his work published. After each class they asked him out to coffee. He went.

He needed to go. He needed to be seen and known. I went with them. I needed to see him, know him, and love him. He was worth my love. Andy had become a celebrity on campus. He deserved the fame; he took the kind of risks that make us all proud.

We have plenty of opportunities to know a little bit of each other all the time. I call it swimming in the shallow end of the ocean. We can bump into each other but not really get intimate. And we can get to shore easily enough if we get a little too close accidentally. That's phantom safety, no-risk living. You don't lose much but you don't gain anything. There are no steadfast exhilarating results in such a fragmented and shut down life. It leaves us all longing for more – we usually don't know what that *more* is, but we are dying from the craving of it.

That more is touch, feeling, and intimate connection, being seen, heard, and known. It is meaning something important to someone you find important and valuable. To be seen, known, and loved is to be somebody. We all want to love and be loved in a way that supersedes the norm. We all want to be somebody to others; we crave it. But are we brave enough to say so? Usually not. We'd rather be dead than be honest with ourselves. We build walls between us, aided by unseen self-created demons that chatter in our heads all day and long into the night.

Nobody wants his or her demons to be openly known. Demons are a messy lot and people might talk. We love to pretend that we don't like messes, or the talk. But if no one is talking about us we feel left out in the cold. We pretend that we want perfect cookie cutter lives free of pain. We don't want to touch into anyone else's messy pain and we don't want ours exposed, or so we think and believe. We have forgotten that pain is a teacher leading the way to unblocked passion. Pain is often our greatest healer.

The art of staying distant is built on a grand lie that won't hold much water in the face of truth, as you saw with Andy's story. It is a successful lie when not challenged as long as it works. We do nothing and darkness prevails. Doing nothing feeds the lie.

The lie says that if we are afraid of each other we will be safe. It is absolute foolery. This lie has managed to keep us strangers unto ourselves and to others because it is perpetuated through families and generations. You stay in your space and I will stay in mine, that's how the lie works to keep you and I smaller than our biggest self. It is a sad and sick lie as long as it is a thief robbing us all of the things we crave most, a deep connection with self and opportunities to go deeper with others than we have ever imagined or dared before.

Do you want to continue to be children of this thieving lie? Think about that. Look at the cost. Decide what you will and will not pay then live within that context.

Now that you have heard about Andy, our rebel writer who openly challenged the lie, let me tell you a contrasting story about a popular actor I dated who made a different choice.

The moment this man and I saw each other, sparks flew between us like shooting stars that snared our breaths and held them captive. Actually, thinking about it in this moment, I remember it starting that way and then becoming more like a blowtorch turned on high all around us. The attraction was scorching, breathtaking, magnetic, and unspeakably seductive.

He was unbelievably gorgeous; tall and thin with graceful hands, intense jeweled eyes, sandy blonde hair cut just the way I liked. I use to collect drop dead gorgeous men like little old ladies collect salt and pepper shakers. I'm not proud of it.

His first words to me were "Where have you been all my life?"

I laughed out loud, fearlessly thinking this a less than creative come on to a woman as savvy as I. And I said that it was a stupid first line directly to his face. I was prepared to walk away if he refuted the fact.

He frowned rather seriously and said, "No really. Seriously. Where the hell *have* you been? Do you know how long I've searched for you? I looked everywhere I went all across the world!"

Unexplored doors flew open and we walked immediately through them.

Our meeting was arranged a long time ago and we knew that right away. It was no accident or chance. This ancient information allowed us to disregard the typical canned politeness common in new relationships. Instead, we mischievously and freely snickered at each other's weaknesses like children skirting sheer abandon. We sited our strengths as if we were giants. We foolishly talked till all hours of the morning, recklessly ignoring the busy day ahead. In public places we caused idiotic scenes just to stir up his far too stuffy and seriously anal entourage of managers and agents, otherwise known as the "suits." Taking full advantage of his star power, we demanded the best of everything and got it at the snap of a finger. We were drunk with each other, completely out of control, and absolutely senseless.

As our relationship grew the topic of sleeping together became a sticky and tense issue. The *ice woman*, as he called me, gave in under the pressure. It was a rare decision. I typically want to know a guy uncommonly well before I take that step. However, as pieces fell into place it seemed a wise enough move. We let our passions play and they played us into exhaustion.

Things went well for a few glorious months, then when the connection moved past lust and into a beloved energy, my sweet actor began to show me something totally new. He was afraid of me, nearly petrified.

I had done something other women had not done; I cared about *him*. I cared about more than his money or his fame and all the things that went with it. I understood him; I felt him smiling or frowning even when we were apart. I knew his every mood and respected them all. To me, this man was absolutely exquisite.

He definitely did not know what he had stumbled across in me. The unconditional lover that drips from my pores baffled him. He began a game of *come here*, *go away*, that made my head spin and then he suddenly stopped calling. It became unusually complicated to reach him. When I did, he had no time to talk. Soon it was his agent, an assistant, or a producer who called to say that he was too busy to talk or to see me… there was a new movie, out of town meetings and those damn interviews he hated so much. They were all very sweet and they were all politely lying.

The guy, who could not get through two hours without hearing my voice, begged me to spend days with him and jet off to places unknown at a moment's notice, couldn't talk to me or see me? Something was clearly off in this picture. Before long my calls were not returned at all, by anyone. This is not pretty to write about, and it may be uncomfortable to read. Maybe you've been here. Maybe you've met such a dance away lover.

We went from "Baby, you're the best," to unmistakable flat line of the heart. Our relationship was officially dead. If we ran into each other within our circle of friends, he'd set up a date and then cancel it later. If he didn't use that method of evasion, he'd send someone in his place to explain why he wasn't coming to meet me himself. I only let it happen two times. On the second time I noted to his "suit", "I'm never going to see him again, am I?"

"No, never," he groaned as he put out his cigarette and grabbed for his keys. "I don't know what happened. He just fell apart." And then the "suit" left. He seemed very dispirited to be a "suit" that day.

Three weeks passed. I'd seen enough immaturity and I was hopping mad. While clearing my place of my actor's things I came across a phone list and schedule. It showed where he was filming during that week. I bit my lip and called him on a studio set at the prompting of my intuition.

"What kind of craziness is this you're doing?" I blared into his ear.

Caught off guard, he confessed that he loved me so intensely that it hurt. He was not able to eat or sleep so work was a mess. He blew every third line or forgot it entirely. His mind would not focus and he missed cues. His character and he disconnected too often and he broke scene before the director called cut. Far too much film was being wasted and the producer was furious. Love scenes were impossible… he couldn't make himself kiss the girl. The pain was too much to handle and he was about to be fired.

Holding back tears he told me that he had gotten too close for comfort and that was closer than he had ever been. He could go no further. It was over.

Thinking of this man leaves me feeling melancholy for him. He showed me spectacular and rarely expressed parts of his heart then ran scared into oblivion. I have only seen him on the silver screen since that last phone conversation and still the sadness comes and goes. It's there when I remember that I've been where he probably still is today, afraid to be loved. It is a dark and ugly place.

Was he a victim of the isolation lie? Yes. He chose his master and his fate. What were the consequences of his choice? He has a new lover, a pitifully demanding lover that demands his very life. He took up drinking heavily just after our split. All that pain had to go somewhere. This man loved me more than he could imagine. What you can not imagine having, you can not have. And only a brave and wise man can love a great woman.

Only a wise man knows to be grateful for the gift given. That man gets more gifts. To the unwise man, gifts are taken away.

What is the difference between this actor and the young man from class? It is the willingness to take a risk, to be exposed and face hidden parts of self.

The rebel writer put his heart and soul on the table for all to see, always going deeper into himself than he had been, taking his classmates with him. He took the risk to be exposed and to be real. We became braver, stronger, and more real as well because Andy existed on and off the page. His mark was left on our hearts. My dance away lover is still today content to drown his heart and soul in the bottle, sharing them with no one, hiding the light that I had come to know and love.

And what did I do when my lover disappeared? I went to the page. Below is part of a journal entry from that time of healing. It slaps of the backbone of rebel writing and the healing within the force. He never saw it.

I miss you. It is midnight, what you always called my howling hour. The bed is empty beside me and I still smell your scent upon the pillow next to mine. I wonder if I should throw it away, hide it from myself, or cuddle it and cry. Maybe I will burn it. I'm wearing those slippers you gave me, you know, the ones I hate that look so stupid... old Hollywood. And I just threw away your shaving stuff and note pad you left here.

Did you need those phone numbers? I didn't. Your movie star friends and rock star buddies don't impress me. Well, okay, that's just anger talking. Some of them are quite kind. Are you?

You're gone and there is nothing I can do about that. The laughter you left here can be heard waiting in the walls for you to come back. Hidden tears drop from the ceiling onto my head. Your extravagance lingers and mulls about me as I dress and undress...as if you were here watching me the way you liked to do. But I can't watch you. You won't ever be here again. I know that now. You loved me, really loved me, and you left me in the midst of that unabashed passion. How very cruel of you, and how damnedably extreme! Do you always leave with such a dramatic exit? Damn actors! All glory, no guts. You leave me to face the horror of my own fear... men leave. Even good men leave. Are you a good man gone sour? Who are you? What are you? I thought I knew. But I didn't know your secret self-loathing part and so I really did not know you at all.

Your secrets were safe with me. I would have cherished them, the way I cherished you. The way I cherished your style, your undiluted laughter and the sensational way it made my spine tingle. The way I instantly relaxed the moment I felt your touch. And the way you wanted to kiss every inch of my body... twice... and then again when you woke me up in the middle of the night. And the way I let you. My god, you were an amazing and prolific man. Are you still?

I hurt in a place deep inside that only the page understands. I come here for comfort, the comfort that I can not get from you. I tell myself that this split is not about me, it is not about your fame or your lifestyle. It is about your fears. The fears you will not face. Really got you where the sun don't shine, don't they? No agent or attorney can bail you out of this one, darlin'. And you can't act your way out of it. Star power means nothing tonight where your soul lives.

You did not believe me when I said on the phone that the fears are your friends trying to get a message through. "With friends like that, who needs enemies?" you said. Your words buried the fear even deeper. Have you buried everything we were together? No, I think not. I think you buried all that you are with me. You know, that majestic self. God, it was absolute magic. No character you've ever played could match it.

You said I changed your life... screwed up your head and spoiled things for "common women." You said you could not go back to common women again, that only I stirred your soul and so you will be alone. At least I made a dent. I think you don't deserve a woman like me... bold, valuable and challenging. And I deserve a much better man than you are. I want a man who plays a bigger game, not someone who just runs the bases. ***I want to hear the bat crack!***

My face aches, my eyes are swollen, and I've just been hit by a hailstorm and have no cover. A tornado is brewing in the midst. Tonight you top the bastard of all time lists worldwide. I want to get over my anger and I will when I am done with it. I don't want to hate you... I hate hate... and you do a pretty good job of hating yourself. You asked me if I had a magic wand to wave over your head and make you different. I don't. Sure wish I did. I will miss a million things about you.

I am sad that you could not give yourself the "banquet" that I am. (Your words.) And happy too. I won't be wasting my time with you or on you.

One of our celeb friends called today. "I thought he was going to make it this time," he said. He sounded so despondent. He called me a great woman. And I am. Smart guy. Funny, you never told me that friends had laid bets. Another secret too painful to share?

I will sleep tonight on your pillow and remember what it was like to be with you when you wanted to be here, before the fear won. The battle must have been long fought, terribly gruesome and oh so very disagreeable; a lot of blood oozing from your heart broken open, guts lying all over the marble floors of the Malibu house. Did your new friend Jack Daniels knock you out so you wouldn't walk into the ocean? That's what I heard. It all sounds messy and yucky to me. And I know how you hate a mess. Your poor maid. I bet she had to sweep you up from the floor and throw away your soiled designer clothes. Must have been disturbing.

Everything about me got into you, didn't it? You tried like hell to flush me out of your bloodstream, but you can't. Even my house keeping (or rather the lack of it) made you crazy and will be missed. This freethinking rebel in me just about drove you wild, didn't she? You came so close to freedom that I could taste it on your lips.

I can hear and feel your heart aching and breaking, and, yes, it makes me quake with sobs. Rivers rush from my eyes and flood down my cheeks. You were just a hair away from crossing the finish line. What a jerk... not the best role for you. Don't you see what you threw away by taking this new part on a long-term contract? I know you are suffering and feeling ashamed and guilty. I know you that well. Let it go. Or face it. But don't hold to it.

Do you miss me? Yes, you do. And you always will. I got into your heart. I got into your soul and underneath your thick actors' skin. But there was one performance you could not give... a lie that pretended to be you here and at peace. You bailed instead of leading me on and I thank you for that. That was painful, but graceful.

You said once that you love being rich and that of all, with which you were blessed, I am your greatest treasure. I was your best shot... you know that.

Is it lonely where you live?

As you can see with my writing, it is raw and grammatically unpolished. Still, it helped me heal. And that was the point. There were many such writings before I felt completely clear.

Exercise: Have you lost a love? Did you finish, get out all you needed to say? If not, go to the page. Write to the one that got away. Let it all out. Here I could not use my lover's name or give you dates, but you can do all of that. Let it rip!

Remember: This lover is no longer around. This lover can not tell you what to say or not say. Your parents are not watching and neither are the neighbors or best friends who play it safe and skirt the surface of the shallow end. Go deep. Go as deep as you can.

Extraordinary Thinking is based on a psychological model within a transtheoretical approach of non-judgmental decision making that is heart based and tender. It's a compassionate, yet discerning, modality of thought that is emotionally self-responsive, response-able, and intensely empowering. We all make mistakes; we miss-take ourselves to be less than we actually are.

But we are not our behavior. We are extraordinary. We remain extraordinary no matter how we act or what we do. If we are so busy finding fault with our behavior, we won't learn much from it. We will miss the simple fact that we can't change our extraordinary beings into something lesser. We can't separate ourselves from our creator. If we could do that, we would cease to exist anywhere in the known or unknown realties of time and space... we would instantly disappear with nothing left to show that we had ever existed anywhere at all. We would be a no-thing. God makes things. God has never made a no-thing.

Taken from The Tender Art of Extraordinary Thinking
Lee Travathan

Personal Notes:

Rebel Writers and The Cosmos

You will write if you will write without thinking of the result in terms of a result, but think of the writing in terms of discovery, which is to say that creation must take place between the pen and the paper, not before in a thought or afterwards in a recasting.

Gertrude Stein

It has only been a week since I learned that several of my books are being published and at least three of my movies have distribution. I have been working around the clock on chapters, scripts, and making non-stop choices about my future for days. My computer and I have been nearly inseparable lovers. The rest of the world has faded away.

The men I typically date are a sad lot today. They suffer greatly within the context of my success and feel ignored. You can find them wandering around the streets of Hollywood and Beverly Hills, a daze-like haze over their faces, cell phones held limply in their hands, lips dragging the ground. They aimlessly dial my number and mutter incoherent messages into the line. I can not come out to play. Poor babies, they are oh so whiney and unhappy. I will have to make it up to them once the book has gone to bed.

A dream is being fulfilled and life is good here in this place. I took a break earlier on the upper deck of my home in the Hollywood hills. I needed to soak in some sun.

Below me on Sunset and Hollywood Boulevards, cars looked like little ants making their way back to the colony hill. I love the view from up there. I see Hollywood flow into Los Angeles, which connects with the ocean then out to the open sky. It does not end.

Sunset Boulevard has always been, for me, a river of creativity flooding through town. Electricity cracks in the open air here. To the west is the strip where all the great clubs are. I love the world famous strip. It is a hot bed for writers and actors. We get our best materials and make our best deals there.

I am exhausted right now, but there is nothing I would change.

Several friends are going to Borders in West Hollywood at eight o'clock tonight to "hang" with Richard Belzer, the comedian and actor. One of them is a fellow comedian. Richard is reading from his new book *UFOs, JFK, & Elvis*. They want me to go so direly (they are whiney, too), but I'll pass to stay in and work on my own material and carve out my own little slice of heaven.

I am grinning to myself. Life is a natural comedy that needs little help. We work much too tediously at it. Last year I came in contact with a man in San Diego while directing a shoot for my film production company, Awesome Presence Productions. He says he is Richard's cousin and told me he wanted to hook us up. I passed on the offer thinking it strange. A week later I saw Richard on a talk show discussing his marriage. What kind of a guy sets up a married cousin? A wild kind of guy, that's what kind. (I know you can't see me rolling my eyes, but I am right now.) I was not impressed.

A few days later I met an actor named Richard Belsar at a cast call for a movie I was making in Diego. He arrived with a cousin bearing the same name as the other cousin. When the two asked me out for coffee I grinned. I didn't go.

The universe has a silly sense of humor sometimes and I never get bored with it. That must have been the plan I came in with - I wanted to be entertained. Plan A: God, keep me amused. Plan B: Come get me if I die of laughter.

I don't know if the man in San Diego really is Richard Belzar's cousin. Thank God, he gently drifted out of my life when I returned to Hollywood. But I do know that the cosmos likes to play with synchronicity in profound and humorous ways to get our attention to something on the rise. Anything and everything that happens to us means something and everything we do and don't do matters in the larger scheme of things. As we delude ourselves with indifference, the universe covers our butts. Absolutely nothing is left to chance. The plans we came in with are so astounding that our small ego minds cannot grasp them.

It is okay to not know immediately why odd cosmic occurrences happen within our plan. If we stay open, listen and watch, the answers present themselves along the way. Richard Belzar's name has popped up in my life several times with great consistency. The page knows why. It will spit it out or something will happen that makes me say, "Oh, so that's the deal. Okay. Got it."

Exercise: Note any synchronicity in your life that led you to an answer and then go to the page and write about the first thing that comes up. Expand on it. Use a lot of detail.

Write anywhere. Write everywhere.
Write everything.

Personal Notes:

I once asked the page, "If Shakespeare were speaking to me now, what would he say?"
It answered.

The Stage Awaits

In moments past the somber grave... the eyes of heaven .. there I stayed,
till dawn would find me
wide awake;
another lifetime shall I partake?
Or drink in light from the crown,
The Home of God
that I have found?

Alas... the gambler comes to play.
Adieu, my friend,
the stage awaits.

Lee Travathan, from *The Early Years*

Personal Notes:

Odd Things That Boggle the Mind

The destiny of mankind is not decided by material computation. We learn that we are spirits, not animals, and that something is going on in space and time, and beyond space and time, which, whether we like it or not, spells duty.

Winston Churchill

Rebel writers have an inside track on hot questions that boggle the mind. Our motto: *Ask and ye shall receive.* Anything is possible in rebel writing. We can pull information from anywhere, from anyone and anything, anytime. The universe is constantly communicating through every source available. Rebel writing is not limited to only certain dictates. It is the ripe and pregnant field bursting with opportunities for exploration.

Accessing those opportunities may mean that you carry a notebook with you wherever you go so you don't miss a communication. That could be new and different, but before long you cannot move from place to place without your notebook, tape recorder, or laptop. This is a good thing.

Rebel writing is open writing. That means the page is open to all resources without limitation and so are you. I will give you an example. Test it for yourself and see what you like about it, then use it as an application in your life.

For instance, if you have a friend who is not talking to you at this time, go to the page and have a conversation with that friend. Even if it sounds strange open your mind and try it. You will be surprised how good you will get at this.

The first time I tried it I got nothing and that greatly annoyed me. The friend in question was important. We had been unable to talk on the phone as she hung up the moment she heard my voice. Whatever I did to upset her, it had to be horrific to draw such a response. A few hours later I went back to the page and presented this question: Karin, why are you so angry with me? Then I listened. Here is what I got.

K: Oh God, how can you even ask me that! At the party the other night you barely spoke to me. It was a party at my house in your honor and you did not speak to me for more than three minutes!

L: I'm sorry. I had so many people pulling me all different directions asking questions and just about hanging on me. I was bombarded. It did not feel good to me either. I learned that I have to devise a way to handle my newfound popularity. People see me on television or hear me on the radio and boom; they want all of my attention. I wanted to spend more time with you. I missed that. Can you forgive me for handling this so poorly? I promise to do better.

K: Well, I don't know. I know this transition is hard for you. Suddenly you are a public figure and not just my regular old friend. You've moved up in the world and I'm still right where I was. We can't just hang out anymore. You're too busy now.

People invite you to parties just so they can say you were there. I would feel used if that happened to me. It can't be much fun. You are not as accessible to me as you once were. I don't know what to do about that.

I guess this is about me, isn't it? I could have jumped into the group anytime. I pouted instead, like a jealous little girl. I see now that I was one of those people who had a party just so you would come... some friend, huh?

This dialogue went on for about two pages and I felt much better. I did not know if the words came out of my imagination or out of our inseparable connection as human spirits in physical bodies. But I was clear it shifted my energy and took away some of the pain. Later that night I called Karin. She didn't hang up.

All day she had been thinking about our "waves." She shared her thoughts. They were the same thoughts I had written *out* from the page. I became an instant believer.

When I read my pages to her she started to cry. "So it is true," she said, "love really has no boundaries." And that is the way I have seen the page since, as a place without boundaries.

I was able to save our friendship and learn more about the impact of my minimal fame upon my environment. I had no idea how enormously I needed that lesson.

My daughter was young at the time I hosted two television shows that made me known in a small, but tight knit area. I also did a lot of radio on the side. My face and voice were recognizable as the controversial philosopher from the airwaves, and was becoming more so with each day. The Hollywood elite courted me, causing an additional stir of much inflated talk. Top people from business and industry and golf pros made their way through my agent's web, showing up for parties given in my honor. The famous sons of famous men arrived to hear my newest words of wisdom, anxious to see the woman who stirred the stars in her hands.

Within a week of the above writing with Karin, my usually unshakable daughter came home from school crying huge alligator tears. A stunned little face greeted me as she slammed the door of our mini-mansion on Puget Sound and yelled, "The teacher just likes me because I am your daughter and the kids treat me different! I don't like it, Mommy! And I am *not* going back to school! *Not* ever!"

My heart heaved and shook in my chest like a heavy weight falling forward. I gently took her book bag out of her tight little fingers and we sat down on the steps leading to the octagon shaped library, her favorite room. She snuggled in and I clutched her, kissed her cheeks and forehead, and listened to her teary broken sentences. I held in my arms one of the most precious people in the world and this was my wake up call from the mouth of my own magnificent babe.

To Kate, celebrities who flew in from California to hang around my house, people trespassing in droves to get on my property and peek into the windows, autographs I signed, free popcorn we got at the theatre when I was recognized, status; it all meant nothing to her. She just wanted her mom to herself and to be a normal kid who was liked for who *she* was.

Little did I know that for years she feared the public would take me away from her. The stress that fear produced was terrible. Kate had lived in silent panic, not wanting to take my career from me. I hated knowing that. It hurt. What did I do to my baby girl? The dialogue pages I did with Karin days before had opened an invisible door that I really needed to walk through. Rebel writing opens energy and clarifies the present moment. This writing had led us to a place of unrestricted secrets and ways to set things straight.

Security services were employed, my property was protected from trespassers, I did not sign autographs in Kate's presence and babysitters were not allowed to watch my shows at my house during work hours. I told my Hollywood agent that I would not be showing for parties just to be seen. He quit.

Today Kate is eighteen, working and going to college. In the years that passed after we got clear that day on the stairs, she watched friends with well-known parents much more known than I, go through the same things she did. Perhaps her greatest lesson came while watching a long-time classmate, the daughter of famed rocker Alice Cooper, handle the attention. This helped her better understand both sides of the fence.

She cheers me on now knowing that nothing could have ever taken her mom away from her then and nothing can now, absolutely nothing. Not a possessive man, (she's seen a couple of them booted out) not fame, not anything. Not even death. If I were an angel, she would still hear, "Are you drinking enough water today, Kate?" and "Thanks for being my kid."

Rebel writers learn that one thing does indeed lead to another. I call it the universal breadcrumb trail. We follow a lead thought or idea and it leads us to another, and on, and on. We write about it and doors continue to open on and off the page as we go deeper. This is the way of our holographic universe. It is a scene within a scene within a scene. We become like children playing detectives in our personal lives and they become easier. All you have to do is ask for the information and know that, in essence, we already have the answers we seek. They will predictably show up either on or off the page. No request is ever denied.

The perfect synchronicity of the universal cosmic plan in which we all participate often tickles my soul and sometimes baffles me entirely. For a long time I wanted to ignore it or, at least, pretend there was no truth to the idea that we planned everything we experience here for our personal growth. As you see in this book, the blueprint of our plan is the security that we have all been seeking. It brings us peace in a seemingly chaotic world.

There is a hidden truth in all that exists. How do you know what's on the blueprint? Just look around, read the environment of your own life and you will see how every aspect ties perfectly to another. That's the blueprint and the breadcrumb trail. Absolutely nothing happens without a reason, design, and plan. There are no coincidences.

I have applied extraordinary thinking; thinking that is not ordinary, and rebel writing; writing that explores uncommon depth, to the whole of my life. It opens me up to magic. Sometimes I like the magic and sometimes I am not so sure at first. Like a new shoe, the plan does not always feel comfortable right away. It may mean that I have not stretched enough to accommodate the new input. But I am grateful for my lessons all the time. Gratitude allows the love inside to expand and meet my mental grasp, even if it takes a while.

There is a sacred relationship between brave rebel writers and the cosmos. We know stuff, unusual stuff.

But sometimes I don't know for a long time what the universe is trying to say because I'm honestly unequipped to hear it. That's when I know I've hit into a really deep truth, one that is perhaps lifetimes old. Perhaps it is a greater truth than what I want to know so I don't want to see the synchronicity in the blueprint. I don't want to see anything that may be complicated and I don't want to follow the breadcrumb trail. The brat child within has control and I've dug in my heels and crossed my arms, prepared to spout out a muddle of big talk that means absolutely nothing! This is real and intense resistance to the truth.

I can only make a switch in perception when I fully accept that everything is actually handled, no matter what the appearances. I go on and do what I feel is intuitively right, and God, the dependable universe, handles the details that I'm overlooking.

Getting to that plateau of awareness has not been the easiest of lessons for me. When I hit the wall, I splat all over it. Each time that happens, finding peace means gaining control of my life by letting misunderstood seeming encumbrances be what they are; synchronicity, God's little arrows that light the way when I don't know where to go or what to do next. In my case God has to turn on massive floodlights sometimes. I have trouble seeing when I am being as stubborn as an ox.

Synchronicity is a series of road signs or a map to the spiritual traveler. Many years ago an unusual synchronistic *thing* involving a now well known actor began to happen in my life that is still with me today. At the time this started, I'd never heard of him and didn't catch on to what was afoot. The *thing* was just a little stir, like a soft breeze blowing through your hair. You notice it, but it doesn't mean much.

Friends, very intuitive friends, in the entertainment business brought him first to my attention saying, "You gotta sit down with this guy! Put him on a show or something. Do something, *anything*, but talk to this guy! Get to know him. It's important!"

I heard his name non-stop as he began to create a bigger wind in Hollywood. The guy was starting to kick up some major dust… but so was I at the time, so I sighed and rolled my eyes when my friends weren't looking. Sometimes I made funny gestures like talking jaws with my hands, and had to quickly hide my hands when they turned their heads back to me. When they were looking, intently, I might add, I'd listen and try to be polite. I'd smile and nod my head thinking, yes… yes... I hear you, and who the hell cares!

They saw something hidden to the outside world that was odd, untapped, and most likely spiritual buzzing around between the two of us. It reminded them of wind passing though the trees in a forest. Just because you can't see it with your eyes doesn't mean that it isn't happening. Pure intuition was talking from their open throats; none of it made logical sense. In the obvious world they noted similarities, and I admit that they were there, but I still didn't pay much attention. I was busy on my own career. I did not want to see this man's essence.

But bit by bit, odd occurrences continued to spatter a fragment of his essence here and there throughout my day in the weirdest ways imaginable. Most of it, I could simply ignore. What I could not ignore got me frustrated because it was all over me like my skin and I did not know what to do with it. Years went by like that.

Then the man made a movie that the world and I could not ignore. It was called *Field of Dreams*. The messages within the film about things left unsaid were consequently essential to the whole of society. From that point on I bumped into this indescribable *thing* blowing between us everyday through some odd cosmic force. Suddenly I saw what my friends understood; there *are* odd similarities that I can't explain.

That never stopped.

Today I've learned to accept it... the *thing*. I know that I can't escape hearing Kevin's name or seeing his face posted somewhere, especially here in Hollywood. I know I will sit down in town to have a cup of coffee and end up bumping into one of his friends that may become my friend. I know I will always feel an odd and nagging energy in the pit of my stomach when the reminder of his essence lands into my consciousness. And I will go to the page to work it out. "Oh God... sometimes I feel so weak and small... you will have to help me." I chant the words until I feel calm.

I've tried to ignore these peculiar occurrences off and on for a long time, but that does not feel brave or powerful when I face myself alone. And if there is one feeling that I absolutely have little patience for, it is that of the wimp in me.

So I face it. He's going to be on television at the exact moment I turn it on, in the papers or the trade news that I pick up without thinking, or I will overhear a conversation happening right next to me in which his name will pop up. That is what is. I will run into a reminder of his essence in the strangest places. In fact, just about anywhere I go represents a possibility for an odd indirect encounter. Each day, usually several times a day, something peculiar will remind me that this man exists on earth.

And so there it is… the naked truth. Once faced, it does not seem so awkward.

I know the story now. Some days are filled with events that remind me of the movie *Groundhog Day*, except that I am living these awkward non-ending situations… *it ain't no movie*! We end up connecting with the same people in the filmmaking arena, quote the same bible verses, or we wear the same style of wire-rimmed glasses. We use the same phrases and gestures often, or I end up with his extras that just sort of wander onto my private set and tell me as I direct, "Hey, that's what Costner would do," just when I need my concentration. I hear that we lean toward the same political party and both wax romantic about America.

The *thing* flows into my family tree in an indirect manner. My sister, Cindy, to whom I am no longer attached, has a son named Joey. His son is also named Joey and his ex-wife is named Cindy. That's a brainteaser. Before Kate's birth, I had considered naming her Lily Ann after her great grandmother… his daughters are named Lily and Annie. It's endless.

The universe is attempting to make a point. I have come to call this odd, amusing, and occasionally frustrating energy The Quirky Cosmic Costner *Thing*.

I admit that there is something within it that I am afraid to see. What that something is, I couldn't tell you. Past life stuff, karma, a simple fear of the unknown… who knows? God knows. And unfortunately I have not been willing to listen to the mysteries in the page. I feel that I will get over my resistance. I just don't know when. I hope it is soon. Things can change in a moment if we relax and let them.

Occasionally you may hit this awkward spot of resistance within your writings. Know that you will, at some point, be ready to see the truth in the page. Trust that. When I am more willing to understand this odd phenomenon, I'll probably roll my eyes, have a long needed chuckle and wonder why it seemed like such a big deal. All the pieces will fall into place and I might wonder why I fussed over it so much. The page is willing to spill it today, but I won't write the words. My stubborn side is acting out.

I rarely take the position of resistance, but it is a position you can take if you really feel you must. Everything exists within divine timing. When it is your time to stop resisting a truth, you know it. An alarm goes off inside your head and heart. In that moment, you must face what you know.

A personal friend, that happens to be a die-hard Costner film fan, has discovered 38 quirky connections between my life and Kevin's that are nothing short of mind-boggling, so strangely uncanny. And I suspect that he has only tapped the tip of the berg. Each day I get just a little bit more okay with this fascinating little *thing*. At times it is even very sweet.

Before I came to this place, I spent many hours praying to God, pleading my case that the man is incredibly distracting and I have tons of work to do. I've spent time yelling at the Pacific Ocean all alone late at night… saying, "What? What! W H A T!" I want a direct sign, an unmistakable sign that leads me to clarity. Peace sings to me in the powerful sounds of the waves when I just let go.

I spoke to a close actress friend who's done two films with Kevin for spiritual guidance, and to get weight off my chest. She has a wonderfully understanding sense of odd cosmic occurrences. And I chuckled with David Brin, author of *The Postman*, about how silly and strange it is as we chatted about the possibilities of making a film together. David sent me a story that I am just itching to get on film. He is a phenomenal writer and an extremely engaging personality.

What Costner did with his film based on David's story knocked me in the head and heart and clearly got my attention… it is now one of my favorite movies. It made me think and it made me cry and laugh. Kevin did an amazing job and did not get proper credit. The critics had a field day. David and I fumed about that and took actions to right the wrong; we did a radio promo. Over 200 people called my production company afterwards… they *got* Kevin. The critics did not.

Just when the *thing* was really getting to be more than I dared to deal with, I remembered that there is a reason for *everything*. I decided to just let go and let God guide me, to let it be okay. My mental hands left the control board. I think God knows what God's doing. There is always a method to the madness.

However, the next time someone tells me I have Kevin Costner eyes I just may belt them. Okay, not really… but there was a time. The truth is that Kevin has *my* eyes… I'm a touch older. Mine are actually a little darker green. And I have never met him, at least directly.

Like I said, it's odd. I even dated a man for years that looks so much like a clone that it's a radical cause for wonder. I still don't understand how that man ended up in my life… and my bed! But I know I could not have stopped it even if I would have tried. Like a freight train heading towards a derailment… I did not have working breaks. Talk about quirky cosmic occurrences!

In photos you can't tell the difference between the two. I see it with my own eyes and I still have difficulty believing it. I was with the clone for nearly five years and I still did not catch the resemblance. Everyone else did.

Truly, there were advantages to dating a Kevin Costner clone. We received amazing service in great restaurants and shook-up the servers until we left. The entire staff fought to get to the table first, filling our water glasses each time we took a sip. They stood in a cluster off to the side staring and whispering. Who was I, they wondered? Peg Bundy from Married with Children, the blonde girl gone red from Crocodile Dundee? Oh yeah, I was somebody famous for sure.

When asked for autographs, my guy and I wrote our names and the person requesting it still did not comprehend the point. "We know you're incognito," they'd say. We gave up trying to explain; it was pointless.

People meeting me for the first time sometimes say, "Oh, you're the woman who dates…" I try to be as polite as possible. I tell them that they are mistaken. It's wild.

Rebel writers know that when these situations arise, it is just the universe trying to get a message through. We know everything has divine purpose. So, as they say, don't sweat the small stuff.

The universe does love to play with energy and consequently, as you would expect, we two ships blindly crossing in the night have ended up at the same place at the same time under the oddest conditions. What that feels like is inconceivable. The best word I have for it is fuzzy… it feels fuzzy inside, the effect of a peculiar sort of déjà vu. It's like you're somewhere you've been before and at the same time, you can't get back there. You're in two worlds at one time, a foot here, a foot there… and you're rocking like a boat upon the ocean. You're not going to capsize, but you don't know why you're there. Still, you can't turn away. Something that you cannot see or hear won't let you exit.

Recently our ships passed unexpectedly on Easter day. Kevin, not knowing who I was, smiled very sweetly and waved to me like the true gentleman that I suspect he is. (Mutual connections confirm that he is one of the most gracious men around.) I returned the gesture. He waved again as I held up a camera that I always carry in my purse and motioned to it. He nodded his head in approval, grinned and posed for me. I fired off the shot.

We smiled to each other once more, nodded good-bye and he waved again. I waved back with a disturbing feeling that I was waving to someone I'd known all my life. The thought flashed in my mind: Maybe there is something to that past life stuff. Whoa… that would be wild!

We carried on with our individual lives. He returned to his kids and I returned to my friends. We never spoke. In the end, I suspect that Kevin was simply waving to a tall striking redhead baring very long legs, wearing a seriously short red skirt that just could not be missed in a crowd of seventeen thousand baseball fans. The guy's no fool.

I may never understand cosmic occurrences, but I can't deny their existence. They are part of our blueprints. That day was a perfect example. Friends so long ago were right; something odd is afoot. Something extremely odd.

I developed the picture and put it on the side of my fridge with some silly ones of actor friends who entertain me while I cook. I pass by it now and then, laugh and say, "What Kev… what?" I throw up my hands, shake my head dramatically, huff and puff, and then go on about my business.

Last week I was invited to a party where he was due to show. This happens now and then. The people who invite me don't know about the *Thing* and I don't tell them. I didn't go. Not going was not about Kevin; it was something I was working through.

Kevin makes movies that shift people's lives and may even transform them. At the very least, they offer valuable insights. Through my past radio show, I've talked to some people who wanted to tell their beautiful stories of transformation and say thank you in print. Like the guy who called his dad after twenty years due to Kevin's part in Field of Dreams, it is his messages that matter to them, not Kevin's fame. The fame is just a thing, a moot point. It is the messages that add something good to the world. That matters. Kevin's work matters. Kevin matters.

Kevin is a light. When we don't stand for the lights on our planet we stand in the dark. Excusing that kind of behavior is a passive action not self-honoring or honoring to the whole. When good people do nothing, evil does indeed prevail. Evil, the opposite of aliveness, has many faces that are not always easy to distinguish at first glance.

In a time when movies are pumped out to a market of Joe Six Packs aimlessly watching films with no message of any value, films that are built on heavy sex and violence, I wanted a voice. Other important people wanted a voice. To have that voice is the American way in action. We hear blurbs in the press all the time about Kevin, but we rarely hear from real people. Blurbs are hazy at best. Real folks just tell it how it is for them. I wanted to tell their important and inspiring stories. They deserve my help so I notified TIG Productions, Kevin's production company, of my intent to write the book.

Complications began. In the end, Kevin's attorney sent a letter in response. As my attorney understood it, the letter basically said I could not tell those stories without being sued. You had to be able to read between the lines to understand that. It was said in the most polite legal language possible. For the writer and filmmaker in me, this was a striking blow. I knew something had gone horribly haywire. Metaphorically speaking, it was as if the attorney was putting tape on the mouths of the

American public. But that's not the way of the film star we all know and it hurt. I started to wonder if Kevin even knew about that letter. My American bones ached and my heart was spinning in my chest like a top. I felt sick inside.

I found the decision impractical and extremely unreasonable. This man does an amazing thing, he makes movies that seriously matter, and we can't talk about it in print? I can't grasp that concept. I cannot conceive of such absurdity! I try to wrap my brain around it, but it just *won't* fit. How in the world could any sense be made of such an unwise decision? The miraculous narrowness of it is far too small for my thinking to accept.

I go to the page and I add my discomfort into my prayers. I talk to writers collations groups and ask for information. I spend time at the beach and listen to the waves, asking the waves to help ease my pain.

How does a rebel writer tell wonderful people that they can't tell their beautiful stories? You just say the words with a lump in your throat and feel nauseated and awful. You remember that, after all, we are the folks who stole land from the American Indians and got away with it. None of us are flawless. You wonder where the disgrace ends. You wonder how you will live with yourself for letting them down, for allowing such a serious mistake to happen.

I said the words, "I can't tell your stories or I will be sued," and then I needed a lot of time alone. The people living the stories didn't understand and I can't help their sadness. I can't heal my own sadness yet. And I can't unboggle their minds, or mine. I just don't understand.

In a county like ours, these kinds of constitutional mistakes have a major impact on the whole of society. We all pay a horrid and quiet price. Maybe the attorney thought his letter made sense. I don't really know why any attorney would want to stop such a wonderful book that can only do his client well.

The letter said that there is a strict policy… and I say that it is a policy that needs revision. I suspect that policy is in place to protect Kevin from damaging books being written, but in this case, it is not wise to enforce it.

I have no validation at all that Kevin knew anything about the book. In fact, I distrust that it was ever mentioned to him, and my gut agrees. When my agent asked one of his key personnel if he saw the letters I sent, she did not get a straight answer.

In general, there is something really *off*... I can't imagine Kevin suppressing the voices of others who have a right to speak anymore than I can visualize him letting his own mouth be taped shut. It just doesn't seem to be his style. He is not a vicious man… or insensitive man, I sense that clearly. He is smarter than this situation shows me; there is a missing piece here. And I think my heart has been greatly affected.

He and I were never allowed a sit down. My last fax was ignored, and someone else from his office used my highly coveted private phone number in my confidential letter to Kevin. So much for confidentiality in Hollywood.

When I became the writer and he became the star, we got stuck in the sand traps of the Hollywood cookie cutter maze; we ceased to be human. The maze is where people with visions that matter, that actually account for something steadfast and worthwhile in the world, are red lighted, reduced to dollars and cents and images. It all becomes about properties and profits, not the spirit of the vision. The mental scope of the maze is seriously narrow and close-minded. And closed minds, just as closed parachutes, eventually crash.

The maze is too enormous to fight outright. It has become an accepted part of doing business in Hollywood. Millions of people walk around every day looking normal while being emotionally and spiritually sound asleep. Most people in the maze are asleep. So, prayer is my weapon against its cynical claws.

Everything in my gut tells me that book deserves to be written and the stories need to be told. The press has its voice; individuals have a right to their voice, too.

I think this is why I didn't go to the party. A part of me is hurting. I have things to work out inside myself, anguish to nurse. I did not want to put that on Kevin's shoulders… and I may have, had I gone. That hurt might have spoken through me in an inappropriate space. The back of the bus is no place for a person of dignity and I don't go there gracefully. The letter from the attorney left me few reasonable options. I write the book and get sued or I don't write the book and regret it for the rest of my life... rotten choices. Hollywood lawsuits are messy, time consuming, mentally absorbing and outrageously expensive. At any of these junctures, I simply don't have the reserves to fight a suit.

I never wanted to be on an opposing side… I never expected to encounter opposition for such a simple and loving book. I want to make the world a better place and yet, I have no peace about this situation. I asked myself why these events pound at me so intensely. I realized it is the filmmaker that is screaming and kicking. She wants her freedom of speech. She wants the good thing done.

What I know in my soul is that better films would be made if other filmmakers had Kevin's integrity and saw how that integrity affects others. Maybe the world would see that what we watch *actually matters*. We are affected. Maybe filmmakers would reorganize their mission statements and try to do a better job with the power they hold in their mighty hands. And maybe… just maybe… we would all numb out less.

When the discomfort starts to be too much for this weary heart, I go to the page for consolation and compassion. I ask that the pain be snatched away. I am like a little girl wanting to be tucked into bed when the dark night prevails and the thunderstorms heave loudly in the gale. I say prayers for peace knowing that I've seen bigger prayers than this answered. I've seen miracles upon miracles. God's not finished yet.

The Quirky Cosmic Costner *Thing* will probably be around for a while longer. That's okay. In fact, after over ten years of having it in my face day after day, I might actually miss it.

Kevin does make a difference. Thousands of encouraging stories are floating around in people's heads and hearts, never being given life and breath. Kevin's made an impression in the souls of the American people that can only be denied by the most cynical of individuals… that I refuse to follow.

Exercise: Go back to my dialogue with Karin. Think of someone you would like to dialogue with on the page. Maybe you had problems with this person. See what you can work out. Trust the process and know that whatever you write is a part of you trying to get a message through.

We all have the same hidden parts. We are all connected. The concept of separation is an illusion at best. We can never be real strangers; we can only imagine ourselves as such.

Also, review the relationships you have. Do you see patterns of synchronicity? Explore how synchronicity works in your life. What odd occurrences and things get your attention? What are they trying to communicate? Go to the page; ask it to tell you what you need to know.

Write anywhere. Write everywhere.
Write everything.

Personal Notes:

Personal Notes:

Listening and Watching

Each friend represents a world in us, a world possibly not born until they arrive, and it is only by this meeting that a new world is born.

Anais Nin

Johanna Bridges, the female lead character in my upcoming movie, has been calling me to the page all morning and I can't come. She pouts and sulks. She practices her dance steps for a scene near the beginning of the movie... dancing is to her what writing is to me. We relate well. She dances to thrust away her pain and to feel her joy and passion. I write for the same reasons.

But today I have to work on this book and she feels left out. Right now she is sitting in a gold and black wooden chair in the far corner of her bedroom looking at a long narrow multi-patterned silk scarf, letting it flow through her fingers as she pulls it seductively with the other hand. She wants me to notice. She is doing this just for me. She is afraid I will start another book after this one and delay the movie.

The scarf is painted with her favorite colors, deep reds, and turquoise, deep blue and deep yellow. She is that kind of a woman, deep and mysterious. She pretends not to notice me, but I catch her looking up from the scarf now and then to see if I am watching. And I do notice. I can't help it; she is so beautiful, absolutely exquisite.

It is her presence, not her physical beauty that attracts my attention. It is her situation and how she handles it that keeps my attention. Johanna knows how to hook a writer. I bet she's hooked plenty in her day, which constitutes endless centuries in our time.

Her monster husband will be home soon and she will be forced to do things she does not want to do. At night she will go to her journals and write out her story of this day for me, once he's gone to sleep. She will tell me how each day ends, I will put it on the screen, and she will go on to a new story with another writer or another with me. Johanna will always find a door, a way to get solid on the page. It is not that she is mischievous, it is that she must express herself and be seen and heard just like you and I.

Johanna will write the movie for me. And she won't want a writer's credit at the beginning. But she will nag me if I miscast her part. She will tell me who to cast before I get that chance. But she won't want credit for casting either. She won't ask for much, really, just that I am with her while I write her story. She will demand my full attention. For this, she will give me her all as if her life depended upon it. It does. Without me, Johanna is stuck in the page and may go unnoticed, maybe forever... at least until she hooks another writer. And that's a crapshoot to see who is alive and awake and who has gone to sleep at the page. Those who go to sleep attempt to put things on the page… the sleep is called writer's block. Writer's block is like a steel door to Johanna.

Now she is happy, sliding the scarf across her cheek with those beautiful deep green eyes reflecting the ocean of her present delight. "Got ya," she grins.

Deep down, she knew I'd write about her if she kept playing coy. I laugh and she chuckles, gets up from the chair in a slithering motion, puts on that moody and haunting R&B way-down-at-the-bottom-of-the-river soul music she loves and she dances the way only she can in those slow easy passionate moves. She stirs my soul when she is like this. And until the monster comes home, she will dance and be happy.

Exercise: Go to the page. Ask a character to come forward. Wait and listen and then ask that character to tell you a story. Don't be surprised if the character represents some part of you or your past.

Why?

L. T. But I don't want to be so different from everyone else! I'm too tall and thin and have an awkward face. And I can't tolerate the small mindedness here. People actually hate each other and hurt the ones they say they love. No, it's too hard to be me; it hurts and it makes me stand out. Why can't it be different... why can't I just fit in... you know, blend?

"Oh, yes, we see. Well, this is a bit of a spot now, isn't it? But what would you wish that we do, dear love? Take you back and have totality
make you over?"

L.T. I just wish it did not have to hurt so much. Was I sane when I made these decisions with creation about coming here...did I really know what I was asking for? Did I have to come in looking this way and being a dreamer and a rebel?

Your beauty is not awkward... it is striking... you needed it to draw attention to yourself. And rebels, who have the courage to dream, dear love, are sacred beings, universal treasures that bring us old angels to tears. You asked to be an instrument of your father's peace. True rebels rebel against the darkness in an attempt to bring the whole into the light. They are the candles burning bright in God's eyes.

Taken from Lee Travathan's early Angel Pages

Personal Notes:

The Universe Uses Every Possible Method

Anything, everything... including, you.

We human beings can be a pompous bunch. We are bold enough, ridiculous enough, and egotistical enough, to believe that there is no intelligent life on other planets. That people who talk to God or angels… and get answers… are just a little, if not a lot, nutty. And that God favors some and not others. All of this says the same thing: Let's limit God!

It is a joke of the highest proportions. And the joke is on us. While we egotistically go about our way, believing in our perceived limitations, God goes about God's business, uninfluenced by our silliness.

Someone once said to me, "I think it very strange that you talk with angels."

My response was calm and curious. "I think it strange that you don't. Why take such a gift from yourself?"

The woman looked sad for a moment and then walked away.

It is odd to me that we subtract so much from ourselves in an attempt to feel big. The entire universe is communicating into our lives all day long and most of the time we don't listen. We can't be more pompous than that. God talks through writers, filmmakers, musicians, children, the guy who pours your coffee at Starbucks, the breeze blowing into your kitchen window… and the dishes in your sink. Maybe the dishes in your sink.

I was in the field of psychology for many years working with alternative therapies that I developed. My base format is called *Extraordinary Thinking* and its most employable method of discovery is called *Partswork.* This method has vast applications - it even saved my life once - and it is a great example of the universe using any and every possible method of communication.

I am going to tell you a true story knowing that a secret of the universe will unfold for you. I find this story particularly exciting.

Meet Gary. Gary is a young man who came to my office in Scottsdale, Arizona, years ago. He was sent to me after other more traditional forms of therapy failed. At the time I saw him he was twenty-eight years old, in good physical health and just had this one nagging problem… he was obsessed with dirty dishes. This pertained primarily to dishes left dirty after four o'clock PM.

The problem was driving him and his partner apart, keeping him up at night, and keeping him housebound after that hour. When he entered my office he was thinking of ending his life to escape the problem. That clearly was not the solution. He heard that my methods were a little odd but he was willing to try one last thing. After discussing his past history and what he perceived as his options, it was time to get to work on a pearl dive. He had never heard of an Extraordinary Thinking pearl dive before and was skeptical. A pearl dive is what it seems metaphorically, the act of uncovering information that will change your life. Here is how it went.

"So what if I can't do it?"

"I know you can," I told him. "Here is what I want you to do. It is three o'clock now. I told you how this works. It is the applications of the old ask and ye shall receive idea. You ask and you get an answer. The biblical box is too small for such a big idea. So, go home, turn off the phone, lock the door, go to the kitchen and look at your dirty dishes."

"This is so friggin' weird!"

"Yes, it is. And it works. We do what works. So, I want you to look at those messy dishes and ask this question…"

"Ask who?"

"The dishes."

"The dishes can talk?"

"Of course."

"This is a joke, right?"

"No, this is your life. The one that the dishes own right now. Do you want to talk to them or not?" He nodded his head yes, rolled his eyes and sighed. *"Okay, you are going to ask your dishes... What do you want me to know? And, What are you trying to communicate?"*

"And if they don't say anything?"

"Oh, they will talk. But just in case I am wrong this one time, feel free to come back and get your money for this session. I will be here till six. Someone can pick it up for you, or you can get it tomorrow. If I am not wrong, call me as soon as you have the answer." With that he left.

At fifteen minutes past four Gary called. He was sobbing heavily. "My God, they talked. They really talked! Oh my God! I don't believe this!"

"Tell me more, Gary."

"They said I have to have all the dishes clean by four or I won't... I won't... or I won't be loved."

"Tell me more."

"They showed me a picture of my mother looking at the clock and panicking, running around the house making sure it was spotless, often she was crying. My brother and I had to be spotless and sitting like little soldiers on the couch. I was around four years old. She had to be well dressed. The house had to be perfect. The dishes had to be done and put away."

"Tell me why, Gary."

"Because Daddy was coming home."

With this revelation, Gary told me the story of how his dad came home one day and everything was not perfect. There were more days like that. Things got very ugly when daddy was not happy. Daddy hated dirty dishes and so they went flying. Gary had consciously forgotten all of this. His problem had been building for years; a hidden part of him was attempting to get his attention any way it could. Using the dishes worked.

We talked until about four-thirty that afternoon. I asked him how he felt. He was laughing some and crying, this time tears of joy. The dishes were not done. It was past four. His obsession was not kicking in. It never did again.

It is completely true that if we ask we receive. It really does not make much difference how the universe delivers the message, it does do its job if we will just let it. So, the page talks, dishes talk, music sends messages through artists. And so on. What we need, we have at our access.

There are many stories like Gary's. I tell you his to make a point and to say that you are more loved than you know. Life may be bigger than you realize.

You might think that Gary's story is dramatic, but it isn't really. In my years of doing Partswork I saw one miracle like this atop another. And the miracles were not unusual, just different. Miracles are actually the natural order of our lives when we invite them. And anyone can talk to angels, God, Jesus, just about anyone. Just ask God to help you and don't try it without him. Yes, they answer. In light of human beings each being as different as snowflakes, the answers will be molded to your needs. That's how loved you are. If you can't believe you can do these things, you probably don't believe you are so loved. That's not about God's limitations, that's about your own.

I very often call God "Big Sweetie" just because that is how my perception of God gels for me. Big Sweetie is like the waiter at the table saying, "May I take your order, please." I am learning to order the very best every time.

Years ago I discovered that I was ordering too small. So I stopped looking at the metaphoric prices on the right side of the menu of life. I share a section of a page from my personal journal entitled, My Life with Angels, so you can see how this got handled. Inside this journal are writings like you see here, a record of miracles that I experience, synchronicities that have become tied together to make a whole, and lists of things I am grateful for. Often prayers go in this journal, too. When I pray, it is not to ask or beg for something, it is to acknowledge that I already have the perfect solution and situation.

At the time I wrote this, I was wondering about my writing career, asking if I had missed anything that could help me move further along faster.

Well, you've come to the page. We kept sending you signals and signs regarding this matter. It is funny how you ask for them and then ignore them... but never mind that, we love you so deeply that we just send more.

Remember that within all aspects of life there is a perfect plan. You decided to write before you got here. So, all of your life we have been sticking tools in front of you. When you were a child we brought that lovely English teacher in the fifth grade, that you will never forget because she saw the soul of you in your pages. When you told her you wanted to make movies from your stories the kids laughed, but she did not. That made you cry... she understood. When she sent a present for your high school graduation, it said in the card, "Now, write a story and make a movie!"

We brought books... always exactly the book that you needed. And we helped you use your anger to write so you did not turn it back on yourself or the world. It was so immense and deserved.

We constantly bring you material... alerting you to your feelings when something happens that can make your voice good for the world.

Remember when Martin Luther King was assassinated? You cried at school and the kids called you a Nigger Lover and it hurt like a sword through your heart. Instantly you saw their shallowness and greed and envy... their misperceived superiority... and their mental innocence, the way God sees it.

You went home and wrote; Martin Luther King died today and a part of me has been born. I cannot be like these people who cannot see his beauty. His gift. I have seen too much and know too much to sit on the sidelines and live in fear. I will leave this place someday and I will go to a place where black and white people live in the same communities. I will not stay here where they are not welcomed. This box is too tight... I have outgrown it.

That small piece changed you. Again your school friends laughed, but you accomplished your goal in spite of that.

Today you wonder about your career. Will your books get published? Will your scripts be made into movies? Yours is not to wonder but to ***know****. The answer is yes. However, the concepts are too big to turn over to any publisher or any film company. You need to take better care of your children than to put them into just any hands. You did not do that with your human babies. Is this really different? Put them into God's hands and we will sychronize you with the right publisher and the right distributor for your movies. It is your acceptance of the done deal that pulls the deal together on earth, as it is already done in heaven. Chance is a human game, not a heavenly game.*

So listen for us, dear one, in the shifting of the wind. And watch for God everywhere, in anything, in everything and everyone. Listen to all things because God speaks in all things. Even in the cooing of your new little granddaughter, God is speaking.

Be willing to learn all you can about your craft and then discover more in what the universe shares. Be open, be willing and love. Love the writer in you, it makes her so happy. That makes you happy and that makes God happy.

Within weeks of this writing, I found a publisher that let me maintain the rights to my work, which are usually taken, and gave me free artistic reign with the work as well. I also found a pipeline for my independent movies that is perfect for me, again offering free artistic reign.

When you stop looking at the prices on the right side of the menu – you stop wondering what something will cost because you know you can afford it. You understand what real wealth is. The universe always says yes and that makes you excessively wealthy. In other words, when you own and accept that your dreams are done, they can be done unto you. An understanding of your personal plan begins to take root in your mind. If you have a deep desire, it is the plan attempting to present itself to you for fulfillment. You do your end and the universe will take care of its end.

When you listen to the universe through every avenue available, you will feel more secure with yourself. And less limited.

In knowing that my books and movies are a done deal, without seeing proof of that, things fell into proper order. I would have done just about anything to maintain my rights to my work, but trusting in the done deal was the most powerful thing I could do.

Exercise: Make a list of your dreams. Are you doing your part? If you are and you are really ready to see them come true, done deal them. Accept that in a place you can't see, they are done. Know it. Then watch for the synchronicity that leads you to discover the perfect out-picturing of your dreams here on earth.

Break open the box of limitations! Pick an object to chat with. The car keys, if you loose them a lot, are a good start. One woman I know who drank too much put a bottle in front of her on a table late one lonely night and asked it what it was trying to communicate. The result? She does not drink abusively anymore. You can try this with just about anything, even a picture of yourself.

Personal Notes:

Learn to Ponder

My religion consists of a humble admiration of the illimitable superior spirit who reveals himself in the slight details we are able to perceive with our frail and feeble minds.
Albert Einstein

The art of pondering is nearly lost to our present society. I find that sad. If we do not ponder our lives, we lose them. We lose them to mediocrity. Mediocrity is a numb sub-human condition that quietly and subtly drains our aliveness.

In the film, *Dances With Wolves*, we see an inspiring example of a people, the American Indians, who knew much about the art of pondering. They knew how to go deeper into life, to explore it with their hearts and souls. American Indians hold deep spiritual values.

Once there is little of Lieutenant Dunbar left, Kicking Bird tells Dances With Wolves that he has been thinking, that of all the trails in this life, there is one that matters more than all the others. It is the trail of a true human being. He sees his friend on this trail and is happy. Kicking Bird is a very wise man and these are the words Dunbar has been searching for… a true human being. His search has been the root of all that he is.

We are all on this search in one way or another. We want deeper and richer lives. We want the steadfastness that comes with them. We ache for it, but we will not talk of such things because the words are so intimate. Mostly, we are afraid to admit to this buried desire. People might laugh.

Michael Blake, who wrote the book and the script upon which this film was based, must be a very interesting human being. In order to write such a story, he might have pondered long… or listened intensely well to the secret life hidden in the page. It is with earnest gratitude that I say this. He's done a grand thing. And we are all better for it.

Some writers, not all, naturally ponder. I'd like to sit down someday and ponder life with Julia Cameron; author of *The*

Artist's Way and *The Right to Write*. I suspect she is a great *ponderer*. Okay, so maybe there is no such word, I just made it up, but you get the point. I suspect her soul is deep like a river.

Rebel writers must ponder. For most of us, it is part of our explicit core. We must ponder, lest we go insane. To ponder and to think are two different things. Thinking more involves the act of attracting a thought and then choosing one or more to consider. Pondering is an active listening, something natural to our souls. When we ponder we listen to the thoughts that are already running through our antennas like radio waves. We pick up one thought and let it lead us to the next. It is more or less an intuitive act.

For instance, I might ponder a possibility of being in love again someday. And what if I pondered this possibility while sitting on the beach? Suddenly I see a sunny day in my mind, sitting on the damp sand where my old friend, Bay, has a beach house in Rincon, California. The tide has just gone out. Then I remember my friend in greater detail and smile. Enjoyable times, now past, place this smile on my face.

Suddenly I am inside the house and looking at the large model airplane hanging from the ceiling in a downstairs room and I adore that my friend loves to fly. I love flying. I can hear his voice and see his hairy chest. I remember his enthusiasm for the book about Tesla, the man out of time. Thinking about his response to Einstein's book about how he saw the world makes me grin. I smile that he is a self-made man who is very successful at his business. I remember the last time I was physically there… and now, I want to go again.

My friend is a clue that I'd like to share my life with a self-made man. Now, this is quite a discovery, indeed. I was not fully conscious to the fact until this exact moment. A mystery in the page is now revealed.

I now have the opening to a movie, an essay, a dialogue with the man I will love in the future, the awareness of issues to work out with an old lover, a book topic, or just a needed key to my life. In fact, the more I ponder this idea the more life I will have to play with.

When I go to the page to start writing, the page will open up and reveal its hidden world to me. It will nurse my rebel writer's spirit.

Many rebel writers are born rebels. For me, it is the heart of my basic nature. The ordinary life bursting with sameness is a horrid and dastardly bore. It is less than what we deserve. My personal integrity and self-honor protect me, not letting me numb out to the ordinary world. That world spells death to my spirit.

Some of us are born chemically dependent upon truth and we will do just about anything to bring it forward and give it meaning. Rebels must give the world meaning. Meaning is our life's blood. We understand that there is no one real truth that applies to all people, but we must find our own truths in the deep end of the water. Pearl diving is our specialty. Once a significant truth is found, we must share it. We must risk sharing even if a few boats on the surface are rocked. We rock the boat because what we give of our lives may mean something to others, to someone, to anyone. And if one person changes their life for the better, we have lived well. We have gone down that path of a true human being. And to be on that path is the most important thing we know.

Some of us are ardently opposed to any sort of dogma or anyone who says that there's only one way to do a thing. We may smile and be polite about it in a social setting and then pound pillows (not people) later. If somebody says our little girls can't play on the boy's football team we are prepared and equipped to fight injustice. We want beauty in the world and injustice is ugly so we must clean it up.

If the rebel writer is female, her significant other is to be pitied by the waking dead and praised and envied by others. She is going to want more out of him than he's ever given; demanding his best, she will expect extreme loyalty and friendship. She is going to take him on a journey, most of which will be recorded on paper for his viewing pleasure in notes left around the house and he will never be the same. The rebel writer will rock his world.

She is there to break down unseen walls and build bridges. She is going to hop on a bulldozer, grind the gears hard, and take it deep into his heart where the good stuff hides. She is the Queen of Sheba reincarnated and she knows she deserves the best stuff of a good man. She understands that this makes his life better. Mean, intolerant, and insensitive men don't stand a chance of entering her sacred world. And forget it if you think she will settle for ordinary sex… it's make love, real go-further-than-you've-ever-been love, or lose her.

But one thing will be certain for the man who survives her high self-esteem; he will be one of the luckiest men on earth. When a rebel writer loves there is nothing that compares. If her advances are returned magic will pave the way. She will live her love from the deepest recesses of her soul.

Rebels in general have a need to know what is true about their world. Their heads are always spinning with resistance to the deceit that makes up the common world. Anything mediocre, weak, timid, or fence straddling is cause for alarm. They pull out their pen and paper or run to the computer as if their life depended upon setting the injustice right. Even a simple thing will tend to awaken something grander inside them. Rebels live in an extraordinary world lubricated by pure passion. They are truly blessed, blessed because they say so, and the universe says… yes.

Rebels live out here on the fringes where I am now. Ours is an extraordinary path of sharp rocks, boulders, broken dreams, and the magic to transform them. God walks with us, and sometimes when we fall exceptionally hard, God, or Jesus, angels, or Einstein, Hemmingway, JFK or some other Great Spirit picks us up as we cry weary tears and says, "I will carry you. We can do this."

True rebels with old worn souls must do great things in this world. We must leave it better than we found it lest we drink, use drugs, or slowly die some other way… it is the only way we can handle our internal self-abuse born from a lack of action. But if we go to the page, if we use the applications in this book and others that love us into being human spirits, we don't have to hurt ourselves with outside forces. Instead, the page will bathe us in our own deep truths until we finally own our Self, our wondrous and beautiful Extraordinary Self. The Self we were meant to be.

When a rebel writer meets a goal, as I learned, it is more important to celebrate it in private with the Great Spirits that have helped you get there, than it is to celebrate with friends. The success of a rebel writer is a sacred thing, like the birth of a child, making *real*; not *reel* love, and the feeling that comes when you know you're in love with a wonderful person. In all these things, you can ponder how deeply resurrected you are and take it respectfully deeper. At the deepest levels we find ourselves on the trail of a true human being.

Exercise: Go to the page. Think about the trail of a true human being. Are you on that trail now? If not, how can you start? What can you do to take a step forward? Write whatever you sense and feel. Nothing in this exercise is right or wrong. Just follow your senses and write as long as you need. Do this exercise once a day for three days. Take it deeper each time.

Write anywhere. Write everywhere.
Write everywhere.

Personal Notes:

Good For You Folks

One's friends are that part of the human race with which one can be human.

George Santayana

Have you ever stopped to take a long and honest look at the people you have invited into your life? If not, now is a good time to start.

The people we call our friends will either consciously or unconsciously give us energy or drain us of energy. This is a hard cold fact of life. I learned to accept this fact the exhausting way. It was my habit to convoy people into my life who were not good for me just because they were present and I felt obligated. I did not want to be judgmental and exclude those who had not proved themselves to me... I was *too* kind, literally. After some near fatal choices, I got the message the universe was desperately attempting to deliver.

Having the right and ability to talk to angels and others on the page gives me no special compensations when I am stubbornly ignoring the words in front of me. At certain times, I've made a mess of my life... divorces, affairs, bad business deals... I know about that stuff. And I know tons about how to choose people in my life from botching it so many times. I know what does not work and so I know what does.

We don't have to be judgmental to be selective and discretionary. Judgement is something we do in our minds about a person when we decide that person is either good or bad. People are not one or the other, people just are. Things just are. The behaviors we experience in various people are not the people... people are not their behaviors, but they are accountable for their behaviors. And we will be affected by those behaviors if we are in their space. Ah! Discretion! Herein lies the line of pure decision.

Writers, especially rebel writers that write out the backbone of life, sometimes forget to set certain boundaries for ourselves. It's as if we go to sleep in one area and we are unusually awake in another. People can fascinate us unconsciously and wake up our awareness by showing us their agendas in an often unpleasant and sudden manner. We shake our heads and wonder where they were when we got involved with that person. Rageaholics and other sorts of users need to be kept out with a mental no trespassing sign.

We forget that to honor ourselves we must make and let people show us their true colors without rushing into a decision about who and what they are and how they apply to our exceptionally precious lives.

There are exceptions, of course. All of us know what it's like to meet someone and instantly recoil while feeling strangely sick inside. We get a toxic rush that washes throughout our bodies. That is the universe saying, "Don't go this way, the price is too high. This person is going to hurt you if you let them in!" Perhaps we had a life once with that person and it was horrid. We retain those memories.

We know what it is like to meet someone, get a hit in our gut that this is a great person, and discover later that we were right.

The bottom line in these situations remains the same. Your life is precious and valuable and so is your right to invite only *good for you* folks into it. This does mean a re-evaluation of the people who are in your arena. How do you feel around them? Do you feel respected? Treasured? Important? I am talking about the friends you have just now. That's where you start and then progress on to the other areas of your relationships.

I am suggesting that you get hard core about this evaluation and I am here to tell you that it often hurts to let go of less than healthy contacts. Why? They are habitual. Giving up a nasty habit can be brutal. Sometimes their behavior is unconsciously abusive, or we abuse ourselves by not perceiving that it feels bad to be near this person. We don't always want to know the truth about others or ourselves. But if we don't face our feelings, both friendly and vile, on the page or off, we are part of the living dead common to our society. They have become numb and often cease to grow. Taking no risks to step out of the ordinary box of perceived limitations will assure numbness. It is an unequivocal given. Don't let it happen to you. You have writing to do!

Two images come to mind. One is of a young lady telling me about a dining experience she and her family repeated often at her grandfather's house in the Midwest. At each gathering a particular dish was served that she and her family did not like. In fact, they encountered it as being repulsive to their general senses from the moment it had first appeared on the standard Sunday dinner table.

Each time it was passed they robotically dished out servings onto their plates, smiled and said how good it looked, placed the nasty stuff in their mouths and forced themselves to swallow it, still smiling. This is clearly something I would not entertain. I'd pass on the dish.

I see people do the same sort of thing with relationships. They swallow hard with a smile and try to ignore the nasty taste. Some folks, due to their behavior, are just plain bad news for your spirit. And you deserve better. Maybe you need to know that right here, right now.

The second image involves a man I know here in Hollywood. Almost everybody caters to his every impulse and it drives him crazy that I won't follow suit. I don't care about the "*who*" that he is... his name and status mean nothing to me... I care how the man acts around *me*, how I am treated. I want to be treated well and I demand it. When he is being a jerk, I say so. Jaws drop and the room goes quiet. It is clear that others wish they had been so bold.

"Do you know who I am?" he booms, as if he is saying something that will shake heavy pictures off the walls.

"Yes, and I'm Lee Travathan, a fellow human being. Have we met?" Nervous folks laugh and he changes for a while, until next time. Life on the rough side of Hollywood...

I know that the man under the behavior is not a jerk; he is a scared little puppy praying that no one detect the man underneath the family name and associated fame. I've learned his agenda and I have established some steady boundaries that may eventually tear us apart. If that is how it works out, I will have honored him and myself to the best of my ability. That's all one can do. Then you move on.

For the moment, he still has a slight chance to redeem himself. However, the opportunity won't last long - my gut won't let me dangle on a thread to any great extent. I'd say he has maybe one more shot to save our friendship and then I'm done.

Why be so clear-cut? You may be thinking, isn't that rather cold and uncaring? It is not. It is, however, responsible and accountable. I waste precious writing time when he is being a jerk. He becomes the emotional roller coaster that I can't wait to exit from. Whether you write for a living or write for you, there are no differences. You are a writer all the same. Your time and emotions are equally as valuable. Your life is excessively valuable. Who and what you are to yourself and others means something important.

Don't waste your precious time making excuses for others or cleaning up their emotional messes. If you let people take advantage of your kindness, you won't feel too good about yourself in the end. You miss your own magnificence while the mess maker parades off to find other willing prey, without a second thought of your well being.

Rebel writers need to honor themselves as national treasures, critical to the evolution of the Self and the species called human. We need to live our value. We don't have to be pompous about it; we just need to own our position in life. It is not better than any other is, but it clearly is not less than any other is.

Written words hold the potential to live on forever. I don't know how long forever is, but I do know our value will never be less than it is today in God's eyes. That's how it need be in our eyes, too. We must see ourselves always in the way we are seen by the most benevolent factor of creation.

Suffering is a self-inflicted wound. That which created us did not expect us to suffer, contrary to popular belief, especially not at the price of our own esteem. It is important to people your world with those precious souls who are good to themselves and to you. Notice that last sentence. No part of it can be dropped out for a successful formula.

My friend and I will most likely drift away from each other, except for an occasional meeting within our circle. He is missing part of the formula. He is not good to himself lately and the situation is not improving. As his career falters, he grows angry and restless… abusive. This means that he is not as good to me as he once was when we were closer. I have little or no patience for abusive personalities.

Things change. And sometimes they never change back… usually you can count on that. There is always a blameless and important reason; it is all just part of our plans together. When people change drastically, you might have to grit your teeth and let go, even if it hurts. Sometimes the universe is letting you know you can do better by calling forth kinder and more loving friends. Remember that they are waiting for you, too. What you believe you deserve you will receive.

Lots of people collect stray humans to cast in their true-life dramas. I did. I was good at it. No, I was exceptional. But there is a cost to pay in all things. The cost is emotional, mental, spiritual, or physical – painful or exhilarating, constituting one or more of these. So, choose what you will pay carefully. Some people are very expensive to put in your movie.

My friend finds himself baffled by my personal esteem. The old games have worked throughout his life and still work on everyone else in the business, and typically, on a social level as well. So he doesn't know what to do with me, exactly. The ability to make or break a career with his connections, he has that, and that is a ton of power for any one person to wield. No one dare offend him in this town. But, you see I dare not offend myself… and therein rest the difference in choices that make us real and accountable for our conditions.

Exercise: Take a look at your circle of friends. Are they *good for you* people? Do they treat you well? Make a list on paper so you make it more real - bring it up and out of the page. Now, make notes on what you feel about yourself when you are around these people.

Decide to let go of the toxic ones… write a goodbye note, leave a message, or just spend ten minutes doing it in person. But don't linger. If they are toxic people, you've done that, and probably for too long. Walk away and don't look back. Let it be done.

Do this exercise until you feel clear. Explore other relationships the same way. When you clear your life, you make room for new and healthy relationships to come visiting. The universe loves the person who will step to the plate and go for the homerun.

Do the exercise without judgement, but do be discerning. If someone is not good for you and you continue to play the game, you will lose. If you are doing it now, you are losing the connection to small bits of your Extraordinary Self in each and every minute. Take your value back into your own hands and love it tenderly. Let more good come to you from the page.

Personal Notes:

Personal Notes:

Know Your Space

I am a camera with its shutter open, quite passive, recording, not thinking. Recording the man shaving at the window opposite and the woman in the kimono washing her hair.
Christopher Isherwood

Today is Saturday. I am taking most of the day off; it is the first time I've played hooky in a long time. In fact, as I think about this now, I can't recollect the last time I threw vigilance to the wind and just let my work sit idle. Passion for the work that is actually the playful dance of my heart often drives me at a marathon pace. As I write this chapter, I am aware of the deadline I have to meet on this book to get it in the stores by fall, but I am also displaced from it at this moment. Today I have decided it must wait, step aside, and trust that I will return to its graceful arms.

I've gone out to meet a friend, Giovanni, at the Starbucks on Sunset next to the Sunset Gower Studios. The studios represent one of the older motion picture studios in town… many a great actor has walked there, leaving their mark on your life and mine. And I like that.

I possess deep spiritual feelings about old and new Hollywood. It's fun to observe the two eras blend at Starbucks while sipping a mocha on the outside patio where old men play chess, writers correct scripts and producers grumble about how they can't get good help these days. It's a hotbed for industry types.

I've arrived thirty minutes early just to see what exciting things will take place to connect me deeper to this space. Movement, a shift of some kind, always happens to me when I sit down at one of these outdoor tables. People naturally want to talk to me and I want to talk to them. It's a great place to absorb the essential elements of this wild town that is my treasured home.

I am sitting at a table near the door. A huge full-length picture of Mike Myers in his Austin Powers garb casually graces one entire side of the tall Sunset Vine Tower facing me to the left. It promotes The Spy Who Shagged Me and Virgin Atlantic Airways. A celebrated basketball player has just smiled to me, said "Well, hello Miss America," and gone inside to order. He offered to bring me something, but I declined. I must be looking fair to better today to have commanded his attention. Maybe my sunglasses hid the lines of exhaustion on my face, or he is just feeling friendly. He comes out with a latte and tells me he'd like to sit down if he had the time… but wondered if I'd be in this area again. I tell him that I frequent the place. He smiles and rushes off in a sweet black Mercedes that seems to roll effortlessly from the parking lot. There is something truly seductive about a car so beautiful. The man wasn't chopped liver.

There is an elaborately painted car with big built-up fins, an ancient Olds, sitting in the parking lot in front of me. It has been hand painted by someone who is not an artist and presents a crude sort of advertisement that captures the imagination. The man who owns the car is rushing around the area between the coffee shop and the studios offering the video of the movie he's just made. He is Dennis Woodruff, Hollywood's most famous unknown actor.

He comes to me, I take the movie to inspect later and he offers to sign the full-page picture of himself in the New Times weekly that I just picked up before I sat down. He tells me that his phone number is on the video. He signs and says he will buy a copy of my upcoming movie when it comes out next year and I tell him I'll call.

He is a star in preparation for whatever comes along. I hear that he's been knocking around Hollywood for about twenty years and has become quite the tourist attraction on Hollywood Boulevard's Walk of Fame. People say that he won't lay down and die when parts grow thin, as some less ambitious actors do. And Dennis has the T-shirt to prove it. You can't miss the guy. The shirt and the car say it all; I am Dennis Woodruff – put me to work!

The two old men playing chess on this sunny day barely notice Dennis. A crowd has gathered around them, watching their every move. Some onlookers have come down from the CBS and CNN studios close by for a decent coffee break and some fresh air. They are Bucky Addicts, a pretty twentyish secretary tells me.

A thin dark-haired man in a nice black suit is writing at the next table. I comment on his leather binder bearing a beautiful Celtic design and he reads me the wonderful piece he's just written about living in Hollywood. He is connected with his space and finds it fascinating. His English accent is smooth and refined. He shyly gives me his card.

Giovanni arrives; we give each other hugs and immediately dive into a life giving talk. It's time to catch up on what pictures friends are doing and what we are each doing now and next. We have not seen each other since we attended a mutual friend's film screening a couple of months ago, the night she put her hand and footprints in the cement at Hollywood's exotic Vista Theatre. We'd hung out for a little while at the after party in a private Hollywood home. It wasn't good talking space, too much going on. Too much distracting Hollywood hoopla filtering through every conversation.

Even though this man holds a high position in the industry, it is nice today to stand above all the industry plastic and just become real people talking one on one. There is really no substitute for that. No one is trying to get a script in his hands or wanting him to put them in a movie, not while we talk. It is calming and comfortable. An added bonus arrives, his brother, Pete. They are refreshing for my soul, just like the first time I met them many months ago. *I do so love sweet men with good hearts.* I think they should be deemed national treasures.

Two hours advance forward almost instantly. Pete mentions that we should do dinner soon and we hug each other before we all have to dash off. This has been a precious time. As we head to our cars we talk about how good friends are consequently important in this town… you can get lost in the fame and fortune game. Real friends are grounding factors for each other while *reel* friends rarely are. Reel friends only want to know what you can do for them and that's all they care about. As Giovanni and I both know, when you have a project in the pipeline everybody in Hollywood loves you, so you'd better know how to love yourself.

A truly humane friend can help to keep you in check. We are all secretly searching for the raft that leads to the far shore, the good friend who will not offer us refuge and comfort and encouragement when our old worn self attempts to survive, but will challenge us faithfully to risk ourselves for greater things.

At home I relax. I journal about how my life is changing and miracles are happening at the rate of three or four a day. Tears of gratitude flood from my eyes. I remember Giavonni's face and piercing glance from earlier as I told him about an angel in my life. He is saying, "Do you know how lucky you are?" and I see his heart lying out in front of me. He *gets it*. He sees the miracle. And for those few seconds we are both in awe. I cherish that recollection of this day.

As I sit at the computer now this piece unfolds for me and I sense my angels smiling. I am doing the right thing with my life and I know it at the very core of my soul. The feeling this invokes is powerful and steadfast. I am hitting my mark right on cue. And on the field of life, the bat's gonna crack.

I came back to Hollywood eight months ago after being gone for twenty years, prepared to claim my space. Today this is *my* town. I didn't have the courage to claim it when I was younger. Then my rebel spirit needed to dig in and stay, but I fought that urge thinking that there was no security for me here. Instead, I got myself into a quietly corrupt marriage that took me far away from Hollywood.

It taught me what real insecurity feels like and I did not like it at all. It had bone-crushing claws that gripped my throat as it squawked like a moody raven. It was dark and nearly hopeless. While others looked at my "perfect" marriage and wondered what I could possibly have to complain about, I grew more despondent, giving huge chunks of my soul to this man daily.

I'd foolishly married an alcoholic in denial and never knew from one moment to the next who would be coming home. Would he be nice or mean? Someone I knew or a stranger? It was a gamble all the way and eventually I lost. The oppressive marriage lasted ten years too long.

I divorced him shortly after I had the strength to scream from the stairway landing overlooking our living room, "I have given you everything else, but you *will not* have my soul!" A very male voice arose from deep down in my center that I had never heard before, or since, and I stopped playing the game that day. I found the security in me that was waiting there to be claimed.

And yes, today, these are my streets and coffeehouses and studios. The clubs I frequent and the fine restaurants that serve me with a smile are mine. And the view from the hill is my massive view. I'll share it. I'm not selfish.

When I saunter along the streets of my hilly neighborhood, I am walking the paths of history. Many seasoned actors built their homes on this hill; studio heads and great directors owned property here. Some do still.

Just around the corner is an old monastery where actors, filmmakers, painters, musicians, directors, and artists now live. It has a praying point overlooking the vast city view. Walt Disney was known to study for endless hours in the Theosophical Library there during his early years. People came from around the world to reside with the angels that are still so unmistakable in the buildings and on the meandering pathways. It has become one of my new writing places.

Writers need to *know* the place they live in, the spaces around those spaces and how and why they exist within them. When we visit these spaces we leave behind a bit of our intensity and spirit. We make the place more real, more alive. We drop our pebble into the pool of experience and the ripples go out beyond us, possibly forever.

I write about my life in Hollywood because it is an obliging life. If it were a contrite life, I'd write about that and invite Virginia Woolf to tea. I'd write out my rebel writer's spiritual backbone with frankness and vigor. Deep down, I know that life here is neither good nor bad, it just is. But *this* life is a record of my existence and it is consequential. It is like no other. Your life is consequential and is like no other. It is worth discovering and writing about. Rebel writers often make their lives their art.

When I am about to make a substantial decision of high consequence, I like to imagine myself to be ninety-nine years old, looking back on the decision. I scrutinize my experience in visual pictures and feelings from various viewpoints of *what happened if…* and then I resolve what to do after some prayer time. "God help me… sometimes I am so weak and small."

The universe will speak through my pictures by virtue of God finding my life valuable. And often I am sent angels, human or otherwise, to push me off the cliff if need be. Occasionally I dig in my heels and resist making any decision when my stubborn part kicks in. But the universe knows my pattern and it is ready for me to act it out. I know I want to fly, but I don't want to leave that which is familiar. I become like a small child though thunder is rolling through my soul. This can create considerable discomfort.

As I considered leaving San Diego to come home to Hollywood, I had dire hesitations. It meant leaving my two adult children, my infant granddaughter, and my much appreciated adopted parents behind. The hour and a half drive between us seemed lengthy in theory, giving way to all manners of excuses, so the universe jumped in and sent a miracle of relief disguised as a famous hockey player to clear my head.

In the deepest wave of my resistance, Wayne Gretzky and I ended up "falling" into a conversation in San Marcos, California. It happened that just before a press conference in his new roller hockey rink was to convene, the television crew got stuck in the huge crowd that came out to see the much respected hockey star. Shotgun Tom Kelly, a legendary LA disc jockey, and I, were the radio personalities present for the grand opening, but Shotgun was suddenly missing, too. Wayne, my camera guy, Peter, an audio person, and myself managed to get into the pressroom early. We could sit around and stare at each other or chat.

Wayne and I started talking about how we miss 100% of the shots that we don't take in life… his father taught him that. He had some valuable insights on the subject. We had a treasured and, for me, much needed exchange.

Synchronicity had raised its head. Without a conscious attempt on Wayne's part he became an angel who crossed my path to deliver a much- needed elbow in my side. I had taped our conversation to use on my Sunday KCEO radio show. When I listened to it later I understood how the universe used him to get a message to me. I clearly needed to take a shot at Hollywood again. This time, yes… this time, I'd let it get in my blood.

I wanted to come back. I know I have things to complete here. What those things are, I could not tell you just now, but they are meaningful, like my life here is meaningful. A cosmic force some say, a benevolent unseen hand, drives me. Perhaps. My job is just to keep putting one foot in front of the other in the direction of my dreams.

That is your job too.

Exercise: Look around your immediate and then your expanded world. What do you find that is special, different, or unique? What can you own as *your* space? Ponder these things deeply with the pen and the page in hand. Make the connection. Write until you feel complete.

"I am Hollywood. I am home. You've come back to reclaim treasures lost... and I will help you.
I have missed you, too."

Personal Notes:

Let Angels Seen and Unseen Help You

All God's angels come to us disguised.
James Russell Lowell

I believe we are free, within limits, and yet there is an unseen hand, a guiding angel, that somehow, like a submerged propeller, drives us on.
Rabindranath Tagore

I've recognized the unseen angels who have abided me all of my life. I openly recognize and know the angels that I can see who arrived in answer to my prayers. When my birth family could not love me the way I needed to be loved in order to feel respected, God sent my Papa Lou and Dorothy Pauletto; the parents I'd always wished for, and Lady Diane Harshman; the loving sister of my dreams. I've discovered God in all things, even in sorrow. But I did not always digest how to use that strength skillfully.

As I matured emotionally, after getting slapped in the face a few too many times, I began to grasp the concept of what the creator is and who and what we are. We are treasures to others and to ourselves. We are *all* angels if we choose to meet our highest potential.

Most of us never actually exercise the immense power we have to love. I am an angel writer and filmmaker, an angel mother and grandmother, often an angel friend and mentor, sometimes an angel lover, and more. True, I'm not religious, per say, but I am intensely spiritual. All of life is a spiritual experience in every breath I take. I seize opportunities to be an angel wherever and whenever I feel drawn.

God helps angels to do their business. The whole of the universe is diligently listening to our every thought and word and is always saying yes to our firm statements. We *request* a new car and God says, "You don't sound so sure about this. Think it over and chat with me when you really know what you want." Or we say "I know that I have a beautiful midnight blue Jaguar that purrs like a kitten and rides like a dream on the wind." God says, "Okay. Thanks for the order. I'll handle it right away. Keep your eyes open!"

Information about what my angels and I call The Done Deal Philosophy came to me through the page when I positively needed to understand why some of my prayers were not being answered while others were. It seems that I was unconsciously doing what I was taught early on. In various ways I begged God to answer the prayer, timidly saying, "Would you please..." Without understanding my behavior, I was putting the universe on hold and binding my angels' hands.

I learned that this is a very unfaithful form of prayer for shy and frightened souls who think they may be punished for their request or may feel undeserving of its fulfillment. My angels taught me to call the substance desired done (it actually is done at another level that we can't see) and get on with keeping an eye on the synchronicity that is the miracle unfolding for my viewing pleasure.

That synchronicity serves both the purposes of guiding us and amusing us, if we will allow our hearts to live in wonderment and awe. Our unseen angels live in the space called synchronicity. They excel within its fine art, arranging meetings, getting us each at the right place at the right time.

An abundance of angels both seen and unseen bless me. I think this could be a true statement for most people, but most people are not consciously awake to their secret lives. The average Joe blunders through each day in that sort of sleepwalk state familiar to us all. If you happen to be one of those, maybe this book will help awaken you.

Writers are often unknowingly cruel to their spirit and need all the angels they can get. First off, they often do not take themselves seriously. They think that if they have not published, they are not actually writers. This is, of course, pure balderdash. You write; you are a writer. There are those that do honorably acknowledge themselves as writers and can say, "I am..." while thinking that the lack of a publisher means that they are not good or deserving writers. More balderdash! Sadly, our society perpetuates such cruel lies. Mentally and emotionally we are babies in this strange spiritual land that is our home.

What you are usually not told is that most publishers, unless they are rebel publishers, will steal your rights, disrespect your talents, and most likely leave you with editing horror stories. It's no picnic in the big houses. They are very much like the big studios are to filmmakers... ready to leave you with the crumbs for all your hard work. Then they want your blood and your first born... and maybe more. They want your dreams... and they want to chop them up!

The big houses are in tribulation with most authors. They hold far too much weight in the book industry and vast numbers of writers are finding alternative routes and jumping ship.

When this happened in the film industry, independent filmmakers stormed the show. The Oscars today are going to the bold bunch, not the stuffy and stuck-in-the-past cookie cutter filmmakers. In Hollywood, even those who work for the big studios, including studio heads, are not contented. Often they are in fear for their jobs, depressed, overly stressed, or just suffering from the old-fashioned suppression that has saturated and plagued the industry from its beginning. Rebels flourish. As a result, we are getting some of the best films we have ever seen.

In publishing, writers are honoring their individual voices more, thinking less about a "marketable" and safe product and more about their soul's journey. Those who are sticking with the big guys are paying a heavy price for that choice. And the winds of change are blowing hard through the rebel spirits of those who refuse to go with the giants. We've got David and Goliath all over again and you can expect to benefit. When the lid is taken off the jar, real writing, like real filmmaking, is free to perform at the deepest levels. New unexplored universes jump out of that jar.

There are a thousand known tales from writers who could not get the attention of a big publisher, but had a great product. Herman Melville could surely ring your ears from the grave about the rejection of Moby Dick. I bet James Redfield has a few stories about his early Celestine Prophecy woes. Richard Bach probably remembers when none of the houses wanted to talk seagull. At the houses, often queries are opened by a college student, stuck back into the SASE with a form letter and sent right back out. No one actually reads the material.

Some writers have given up and some went on to be best selling authors with a small rebel press. The big houses that wouldn't talk to them before become suddenly interested when they see dollar signs.

Most big publishers reject or never see 90% or more of materials they receive. It is a silly game that has been played for a very long time. When a book is accepted and does well, it is the house and the booksellers that come out ahead. The writer is almost always underpaid and commonly mistreated. Rarely this is not true, so rarely that it barely need be mentioned.

If you plan to publish your work, I suggest that you work with your angels first. Go into a quiet space and call them forward, seen and unseen, and claim the deal done. "I am a published author and my book sells well to my satisfaction." Don't beg as we have been taught, accept the gift now and be grateful now. Know that the universe is not attempting to take forward movement from you, it is doing all it can to give you what you will accept. It is on your side, remember?

Walk by faith, not by sight, as a general rule for your writing life and your life outside the page. When you walk by sight you do not indisputably own your true power. The universe knows you're better than that behavior. So it puts a book like this in your hands to make its point, uses some other wake up call, or angel.

Only when we stand in a state of acceptance and gratitude can we sufficiently actualize our dreams and be happy. Sometimes people get one or the other, but rarely do they get both unless they have a supportive spiritual understanding and foundation for their lives.

Those who beg God for the prayer to be answered may be showing a formally unrecognized spiritual insecurity fostered by society. Groupthink is often a dangerous, at least hurtful, mental device. When the authority of society is stronger than the rule of your personal truth, you may be in the red flag zone. Groupthink does not produce great and effective rebels or critical and raw writing that runs up and down our spines like lightening. Group thought is its own box of suppressive limitations, much like big publishing houses and big studios that are unable to respect the talent they designate to be in print or on film. When a book like The Celestine Prophecy is overlooked, or a film like The Postman is brushed away like so many grains of sand from our shoes after a day at the beach, something is malfunctioning in our spiritual values system.

I am not saying that the distressing heavy weights of the industry are doing anything wrong. They are not… they are just doing what they do. It's what they know to do. You can not typically teach old dogs new tricks or get a dead horse off the ground on its own. The system is difficult at best to get around in or change. So, we must see their activities as opportunities for personal change and for the evolution of the species, as a whole, something to overcome. And we don't need to fight them. We are not bound to the game.

The advances in small publishing and global net distributing are rocking and shaking the big houses little by little. Still, be aware and mindful of your position if a big house does come calling. I'd hate to see you lose the rights to something you've made for a check that tempts you, only to learn later that you won't be promoted or well respected. Careful of the dangling carrot. Don't let it hit you in the eye and don't choke on it.

Several friends of mine are now or have been best selling authors. Their stories make my toes curl. One is under contract with a super heavy heavyweight, one of the biggest. They tell her what she can write, how, and when. She no longer owns her rights to her "babies." Her calls are not returned when she needs help and her agent plays the same record. This is a common complaint in the industry. That's, in a word, *sick*.

Where I have all my rights and full reign, she and her family suffer. No attempts are made to promote her book if sales go low. It sits on the shelf and that's about it. She can not go with another publisher, as her contract won't allow for that. She's stuck and thinks it has to be this way. She does not have the rebel spirit's fire. I feel sad for her plight and she is not strong enough to break her ties with the giant.

I may write fifty or more books in my life if time on this earth and elements allow. But if I contracted with a big house I could be certain that only a small number would ever be published. What was published could be severely altered and I'd have to forfeit most of my rights if not all. Not a good deal for this rebel spirit.

I have a young friend who is a genius with rather severe learning disabilities that both complicate and open his world. He is a rebel writer and budding filmmaker who is loved and supported by his entire family in that rare way that we all wish all kids were loved. It is an extraordinary thing to see. His name is Neil Lee Thompsett.

At thirteen years of age, Neil wrote his first novel entitled, *Becoming Human*. It is a science fiction thriller filled with dangerous new ideas that offer a truly original look at mankind and at our place in the universe. It is a must read book for any thinking person.

I was recently with Neil and his family at their home in Beverly Hills. I had a lot of questions for this young man… he fascinates me.

Two of his favorite movies are Waterworld and The Postman, as you might suspect, and he *got* the messages in them both. This kid's going places! Most adults didn't get the messages in those powerful films. He is encouraged by his family to make his first short film, in the works at this time, and I encourage him, too. We can't let this kind of drive, creativity, and talent, fall through the cracks.

As I sat around the pool talking with Neil and his father, I was beaming inside. One more rebel writer hits the deck running and we are all better for it. As the back of Neil's book says, "When a gifted child summons up the discipline to overcome a serious learning disability and write a full-length novel, perhaps it's important for us to find out just what he is trying to say." Yes, indeed! Neil did not go with a big publisher. Wise move, Neil. His voice was not muffled.

There are many books on the subject of publishing. Go to the bookstore and ask someone to take you to the proper section so you can begin to educate yourself about the industry. If you are interested in self-publishing, check books written by Dan Poynter. He knows all avenues of the publishing business and is a great guy to talk to if you need extra help. Look at all your options on the bookstore shelves and check the net as well. Dan can help you there likewise.

Then, before you do anything with your manuscript, work with your prayers and angels. Watch what happens in your outside world when you claim your book published. And remember the universe has your blueprint. You are safe and secure even in the midst of pain or disorder. It has all the decisions you came in alongside and as soon as you accept what is rightfully yours, it will go to task making your dreams come true here on earth.

Advance the timing through prayer or meditation, whatever you call your designated time. If you have a strong urge in any direction, it's leading you to something already in your plan, a done deal. Then appreciate that the universe sincerely works in mysterious ways… watch the synchronicity in your life escort you from one step to another. Stand in gratitude for each step on the way to your goal and know the deed is done.

You might want to rent and mindfully watch the movie, Field of Dreams, for added inspiration. Remember God talks through all open avenues and this film was one of them. As an optional exercise, you could make notes from the film each time you capture a piece of synchronicity as it floats by on the screen. This will help you learn to see it better in your own life.

I'd also advise you to read the book, *Building Your Field of Dreams*, written by Mary Manin Morrissey. It is at your bookstore or you may order it. Mary is an awesome woman with a visionary heart and a majestic gift she gives to the world. She knows what it is like to watch dreams come true first hand.

Personal Notes:

Write "Out" Your Love Story

It's a funny thing about life; if you refuse to accept anything but the best, you very often get it.
W. Somerset Maugham

A few years ago I realized that I could not do intimate relationships the way I had always done them. A shift occurred in my perception and I suddenly become extremely selective about men. This changed my thinking and life events dramatically.

It means that I am detached more often, but when I am with someone, it means I seriously want their companionship. I am not just spending time hanging out. The results have been equally as dramatic as the decision itself. Men know me to be serious about how I spend my time, so they feel designated and important when I choose to be with them.

Even though it may not look like it to the naked eye, I am writing *out* my love story into life. I go to the page and it captures the hidden story on paper for me to see privately.

The shift is a form of communication. It is telling me that the time of settling for less in men than what I deserve is over. I've hit an invisible tolerance point and burst through it. Less men in my life... yes. That's a certainty I live with. Where there were many, there is now only a precious few. And that is not invariably comfortable. Old habits die hard... those aren't just words. But when I do bring a man into my life, he is the cream of the crop and I know it well. That makes me feel guiltless about myself; I am not using the man for my entertainment so that I won't be alone. Consequently there is a balance present that I did not have before. When I heed the counsel in the page I am inspired by what I ascertain and live.

Most men and women I know are willing to settle for less in a partner than what is naturally good and healthy for them. They do this for diversified reasons; so the frowning night won't be painful or uncomfortable, so they will have personage to be out with and not alone, so they are not mentally indexed by others as terminally "single."

I can understand these compromises and have compassion; I lived them, too. But I cannot now and I won't by any chance be able to again. The price is too dear. I have wasted years with the *wrong* men who did not deserve my attention. I am a woman who loves profoundly and loyally. Sometimes that kind of love was not appreciated because the men I chose would not let themselves own it... they did not feel worthy and deserving.

Writers, and especially rebel writers, need to respect their alone and quiet times. We need to make decisions based on the long-term effect of our choices and not our fragmented feelings in the moments of attraction. By taking the extra time to look at the long-range effect someone may have on our mental and physical environment, we automatically click into our intuition. It is a luxurious guide that is often savagely abandoned.

Since everything we do and don't do matters in the long run, intuition is the best place to start when making a choice. Go to that place in your mind where you are older and look backward before jumping forward. This is a true and valuable act of self-honor.

Over the last few years I have developed a new philosophy about relationships that seems to make my life easier. I now believe that most relationships are filled with missed opportunities for valiant tenderness and subsistence. Relationships, like the rest of our "common" lives, have been looked at as something to do and not avenues into beingness. Many are functional, lacking aliveness and spontanitity. Some are so dysfunctional that they easily qualify as physical and mental destructo-derbies. I believe that the best relationships are those filled with depth, compassion, and a penetrating longing towards intimacy.

People, in general, do not take full advantage of their relationship possibilities. They do not understand that they can. This rips at my rebel writer soul. Why? I've seen glimpses of magic and I've had moments of magic with a couple of my men in the past. I know that those moments will stay with me forever.

They are pure enchantment; not something contrived as a form of manipulation. In those moments God loves God through human beings.

Others crave it, this same kind of magic in their lives, but either don't know how to witness it or don't believe they can have it. Sometimes they are with a partner who is not open hearted and open minded, a sure-fire recipe for tragic and painful disappointment.

By going to the page and writing *out* my love story, I already know what I have to offer a wonderful man when he shows up in my space. I know that I first need to develop a powerful friendship that I can count on… one that will not drift away too easily… one that matters to us both. Within that friendship I can set free those magic moments simply by considering the thought: What more could I do to bring happiness to this man's life and my own? I will journey to the page and take the thought as far as I know how to, engaging the love story as it unfolds. If I have wisely picked the partner, it will unfold in the world apart from the page quite beautifully.

My present love story unfolds gently in miscellaneous ways. Sometimes it lays itself out before me in a dialogue with someone I have not yet met, in the form of poetry, in a letter to that person or from them. I have a firm recognition of my guy's essential nature, though I may not want to know his face just now. I do know that he is feasibly in the same business as I am so that our creative drives can be mutually understood and respected. I have dated men outside the industry and I found us incompatible. They could not relate to my passion for the page or for filmmaking. We lived in contradictory worlds.

There is a comfort in going to the page to write out your love story. You learn about yourself, what you will and won't do. How you will and won't respond to various ideas that may be presented. What you will and will not indulge in behaviors. It is good to know these things in advance; it makes you feel solid and strong.

I know a filmmaker that "goes with the flow." He's exceptionally unhappy. We recently talked about this and I realized he has absolutely no clarity about what he wants in a relationship. Instead, he floats passively from one woman to the next, sleeping with this one and that one; young starlets he meets in a bar, looking for a door into the film world. He then complains that he feels empty inside and used. He does not know why he feels so empty, he just knows something is missing in his otherwise perfect life.

Sometimes going with the flow is a concept misused to promote a lack of accountability. This man desperately seeks a mate, a friend, a partner, but does not realize that he must make himself his own mate first. He is completely unaccountable to change within the situation.

We recently talked about a marriage ceremony I had for myself with friends and family. I married my commitments to my dreams and to myself. I did this in a formal ceremony involving an ordained minister with all the frills of a typical wedding ceremony. It was grand and extremely powerful. Not a dry eye was to be found in the room. No visible bridegroom was present, but on the unseen level we all knew that in spirit he was present. Who is he? I don't know. But the universe knows that somewhere out there he is looking for me, too. And it knows that if I am serious, indisputably serious about another human being, I'd better get myself in check first.

My friend asked, "Is it really necessary to go to such great lengths to make a point to yourself?"

Maybe for some people the answer to this question would be a resounding no, but for me, it was how I had to do it. I had to put myself on the line in a manner that would not allow me an exit door into the hallway of excuses. I had to hear myself speak the words of commitment in front of people close to me. I had to feel the energy of the experience run through my body. I needed to ground myself in the knowledge and awareness that when I did meet the man I want to be with, I will be with him in the wisest possible manner. I needed to face my own deepest fears and truths.

My friend does not understand such radical and innovative self-honor… he is intellectually content with the ordinary world and its boxes of mediocrity and limitations. I am not. He will continue on the same journey of unhappiness in relationships because it is easier than actually doing anything productive about his pain. I have chosen another journey, one of courage and exploration.

As a rebel by nature, and a rebel writer, I may always conduct my life in a manner that fits somewhere outside of stagnation. It is critical to my happiness and spiritual survival. And so my love story is alive in and on the page. I know the man I will end up with quite well without meeting him physically, as he is always present in the page. I can talk with him anytime and receive communications. There is magic in this process. Aliveness.

When you are ready, go to the page that you may meet your love story head on. If you already have a wonderful soul in your space, know how blessed you are. Express that gratitude openly and use this chapter to deepen your relationship. If you have yet to meet that wonderful essence, meet him or her on the page. The essence is waiting for you to come visit.

Below is writing from "my guy" to me taken *out* of the page. Read it over, ponder it, try on the feeling for size and then go to the page yourself.

I worry about you not eating enough, and not often enough. It is difficult at times, from this dimension of pure thought and timelessness, to encourage you to leave your work and go to the kitchen. I love it when you actually get my message and move in that direction. I know you can't see me, but I am jumping up and down in the page and clapping.

Watching you work is like watching magic happen. This thing you have with magic, this relationship, I understand. We creative mad people must stick together. I watch you like I listen to a symphony. It is the same when you sleep... magic.

There are days when I am impatient to see you physically. But this communication helps. Can you see me? Do you know my face? I think you choose not to see me... you've been so hurt in the past. Telling you that I have not come to hurt you will not help. Only when you meet me physically and see this for yourself over time will it matter. But you are brave enough to meet me here, and that is bold. You are strong. Not being willing to see my face, like the way you see Johanna's face, may make it more fun when we do meet on the physical. As soon as you meet me there, you will know who I am to you.

I know that you know my voice... maybe not the sound, but the feeling is certain within you. I laughed at you laughing at my silly voice and me a few days ago before that important Hollywood meeting. I am so tickled to see the powerful writer and filmmaker blatantly take command in a situation, knowing full well the little girl that resides within your soul. I love your indie spirit!

I have dreamed you all of my life. I look forward to being with you in the world outside the page. Know what I am thinking... we are good together. I know that clearly. As you say, I'll make room for you in my life. And I understand your passions and respect them. I will not say that I love your essence and then try to change you.

The candle is calling me to let it rest its wick and the bed is calling me to slumber. I worked hard today, well, not really hard, just long. I will miss you as you slumber, maybe. Who knows... maybe I will be right there with you... that is a nice thought.

Do you think your book will help people break through limitations in common thought? I pray it will. Much communication is wasted on the hearing deaf.

Sweet dreams my beauty. I am always here in the page.

Rebel Writers, Judgement, and Forgiveness

Man must evolve for all human conflict a method which rejects revenge, aggression and retaliation. The foundation of such a method is love.

Martin Luther King, JR.

Rebel Writers need, for the sake of sanity, to write out their passions, all passions. All emotions. They write them *out* so they do not need to act them out into the world to any extreme degree. The act of rebel writing clears the soul immensely, creating a whole and positive effect. It is a way to "do" life so that life is not doing you. It may emerge thunderous at times, but it is an effective method of bringing peace forward within others and us. Rebel writers write for everyone, whether they are conscious of that or not.

Within the pages of this book, you've read some things about my birth relations that are not inordinately attractive. They were complex for me to write about and maybe a little perplexing for you to read. All the same, they are profoundly significant. Perhaps the most important aspects of the pain I endured at the hands of emotionally precarious personalities, those who permitted their emotions to drive their actions, were the lessons of judgement and forgiveness.

When we judge someone; make the person wrong instead of their behavior wrong, or we refuse to forgive others or ourselves, we hurt the sum total of the species. This cannot be seen with the physical eye typically, but the effect strikes at the center of our beings.

This is why we are better off to write our hearts *out* then drop the judgements and forgive. All health, emotional, physical, mental, and spiritual begins with self-respect, self-honesty and self-honor.

A couple of days ago I spoke to my supposed "birth" father and my adopted father in the same morning. This has never happened before. These two men are worlds apart in reasoning and it boggled my mind a bit to hear the two opposite voices and attitudes so close together. It was also the first time I told my birth father about my adopted dad. I received no reaction, really. I expected a house to drop on my head… but there was nothing noticeable. It didn't seem to mean anything to him once the words were out.

I've never really known that my birth father is my actual father… it's hard to say. During the brief time I lived with my birth mother, she told me that he is not my father.

This gave me a much-needed explanation of why I don't resemble the rest of their children. I do not think like the bunch or act the same. I am a complete misfit in all ways possible. My mother and I bare no resemblance… also odd, while my birth sister is a duplicate of my mother. I think mother told her truth to get it off her chest, while I was glad to make some sense of very old unanswered questions. It's difficult to live in a family you don't resemble, or so it was for me. I was never allowed to forget my place last in line as "just another mouth to feed."

I called my "birth" father to inform him about this book. I told him that I'd altered some of the material to protect the privacy of those noted and kept the point clear. He understood. I said that I needed to make it possible for others to heal using my story. Again, he understood. I did not recognize an emotion one way or another. He said he was glad for me that I was publishing the material. This is the best he is able to do.

Years ago I could not have made that call about my book. The pain was too great. Until I divorced myself from this toxic family, I could not heal. When I did take such a bold action, I could finally talk to this man who hurt me so badly and forgive him. The truth is simple, he did what he knew to do when I was younger and he does what he knows to do today. He has never been educated about healthy emotional living.

Is his way of loving sufficient for me to feel loved? Absolutely not. I'm not good at monotone relationships. And so I asked God for another father, which I have been given, who does leave me with the feeling of being loved. Does this mean there was something wrong with the other one? No. Just something missing. That was not good or bad, it just was what it was and is.

Using writing to heal is a phenomenal thing. In order to heal my Grand Canyon sized wounds with all of my birth family; I needed to write ten journals full of letters to family members that were never sent. I did this over a period of years, slowly but steadily. The activity was heavier during the last two years of the journals, as this was the hardest time to bear their excessively damaging behaviors.

I wrote in the journals as long as it was not possible to be heard off the page by the people I wrote to. They committed atrocious and disgusting misdeeds against me, mostly because I am consequently different. They assassinated my character in the interior of the family with their horrific lies. In our society, as in my birth family, those who are different are made to pay for breaking the block-shaped box that the fearful live within. No one is suppose to color outside the lines and I did it naturally! Oh horror of horrors!

The pages healed me. In those letters I purely let all the toxic energy flood out and began the process of true forgiveness and prayerful understanding beyond judgement. I am the first to accept that what these people did in the name of love was dismal… exceptionally wrong. But in all dire honesty they did not then and do not now know any better way. It is insane to punish people for what they do not know or understand.

Your pages are personal until you say otherwise. Let your anger surface there and shred the pages later if you feel you need to. But do not keep these powerful energies inside. Free them to the light of understanding.

Always give yourself permission to destroy your pages when you are done, especially the extremely personal pages, and you will be more open to the page at the beginning. We all need our privacy. We need to have our secret world; it is our birthright.

I am presently writing letters in my current journal to people that I have discomfort with. It is the tiniest spatter, but each speck is important. I write to anyone about anything in my private pages for the same reasons I wrote to my birth sister and brothers. It helps me heal. This act of self-respect will continue until I feel clear on the issue. I've written letters to Kevin Costner regarding my disappointment with the book situation that will never be seen by anyone but me. We do what works. It does not need to be logical. Logic just gets in the way of healing.

Rebel write the backbone out of your feelings already waiting in the page for expression. Go as deep as you can go and do not judge yourself for what you write. Let it rip and then let it go. Be angry about a behavior, not a person. Judge the behavior all you want, often it is essential to change in the world. And then forgive them both. Forgive yourself for ever believing that you and your behaviors are one in the same. Set yourself free.

I spent the evening with actress and dear friend, Sally Kirkland, at a spirituality-based gathering last night. Yes... Hollywood has a spiritual community well hidden in the glitz. The issues of judgement and forgiveness were discussed. As I drove home, I realized that rebel writers need to drop judgements of people and forgive *everything* that they may keep giving to themselves and the world. It is a way to keep the channels of light flowing through our spirits, as well as a way to remain healthy, that we may continually expand our writing.

I thought about the evening and what it meant to me. It was a good night, indeed, and I came home smiling. I appreciated how Sally and I could be so present for each other, as we have been in other times and places when she's been a guest on my radio show or I've bopped around the country promoting one of her films over the past year or so. The spiritual connection between us has been present since we first got to know each other; it is a treasure. I respect that.

Within this evening, I was going through some very unspecified raw ocean-like emotional waters during a particular clearing exercise, and Sally encouraged me to let it be okay to have the feelings, even if they made me nervous. We held hands until I got my frail self through the energy. This made a world of difference, to know, to see, and feel that someone I care for cared to render her love. I could feel her center so effortlessly.

Without words we both know that even when we don't see each other for a while, spirit is still at work in our lives and a cycle will come around, a door will open. I'd not seen Sally in three months. I missed her and had given up on reaching her, but that old universe is wise and indulgent so it opened a door for our schedules to blend. My daughter got to talk to Aunt Sally on the cell and it made her night. She had missed her, too. All was well in the end.

Things open up when rebel writers write. Did the doors open because I am writing this book? I suspect it had something to do with it. I am in that space of action on behalf of my dreams and that is potent. All sorts of miracles can happen when you clear your channels and act from boldness and commitment.

Sally was one of my angels last night and I pray I was one of hers. I can still see her smile and feel her hand today. My heart is grinning. Life can be this simple.

Exercise: Who do you need to stop judging and forgive? Is it you?

Go to the page and write the first things that come up when you consider the thought proposed. Do not analyze; write.

Now, write a letter to someone with whom you have unfinished business. Remember that they are not going to read this letter, so do not hold back any emotions. Let them flood all over the page. Do as many of these letters as you need. Now it is time to forgive.

Personal Notes:

Writer's Birthrights

To become the spectator of one's own life is to escape the suffering of life.

Oscar Wilde

Without this playing with fantasy no creative work has ever yet come to birth. The debt we owe to the play of imagination is incalculable.

Carl Jung

You have rights to your soul, spirit, imagination, creative endeavors, voice, intuition, thoughts, ideas, and choices. You have the right to write.

If anyone ever told you that you couldn't write… a grade school teacher, a parent, your own inner critic, they were inaccurate. Not only can you write, but also it is your birthright to do so. You did not have to earn the right or earn the magic within it; you were born with these possessions. You possess the ability to listen to the page and record its communications.

If it feels like you are unable to slow down your logical mind to get to the goodies, just sit comfortably and focus on your breathing going in and out. Pull in peace in the in breath and push out chaos on the out breath. If your mind wanders, just pull it back to the focus on the breath. This method is simple and relaxing for the writer within.

All day long we are bombarded with ordinary messages that exact small to large bits and pieces of our Extraordinary Self. When we repeatedly tell ourselves we cannot do a thing, we cannot. Our words are powerful self-fulfilling prophecies. They thunder through the universe and come back to us as results.

I want you to know that you *can* write. Your were born with the talent to do so. It is healthy for you to write. And each time you write and do not judge it, you will live to write closer to the edge of wonderment. You will both amaze and amuse yourself if you give up the judgement that has been swallowing you whole. It has not allowed your writing to be free.

This chapter is short and the exercise is extended and freeing. I know this simple collection of words will shift your life if you let them.

Exercise: Make a list of all the things you do not let yourself do or have. Ponder it for several days, adding to it specific observations that indicate transformations in perceptions.

You will notice how you keep yourself in the box. Write about what it is like to abandon the box.

Good ideas and innovations must be driven
into existence by courageous patience.
Admiral Hyman Rickover

Find Your Way

It is not the critic that counts; not the man who points out how the strong man stumbled or where the doer of deeds could have done them better. The credit belongs to the man who is actually in the arena; whose face is marred by dust and sweat and blood; who strives valiantly; who errs, and comes short again and again, because there is not effort without error and shortcomings, who does actually try to do the deed; who knows the great enthusiasm, the great devotion, and spends himself in a worthy cause; who, at the worst, if he fails, at least fails while daring greatly.

Far better it is to dare mighty things, to win glorious triumphs even though checkered by failure, than to rank with those poor spirits who neither enjoy nor suffer much because they live in the gray twilight that know neither victory nor defeat.

Theodore Roosevelt

The last three days have been wacky and I have been "agreeably edgy." That means that most people going in and out of my house this past weekend did not notice that I was quietly destined to go goofy and flippantly eccentric at the drop of a hat. I was in my own creative world. Nothing seemed to be working right outside that world until I remembered it is *all right*.

My friend Irene noticed... she will let me snarl and be grumpy around her, or as odd as I need to be. She's known me so long that she is aware it is deserved big talk that has to come out somehow. I am venting. I fuss and fume, get all worked up, and she chuckles with me later. Once the punch wears off we both get positively dippy. Stupid jokes flood from my mouth and I can't stop them, but Irene never tells me how dumb they are. She just laughs. I love that about us. Our friendship lasts despite my growling and big talk about how provoked I am. It survives my ditzy jokes. What more can a friend ask?

She came to help with cooking, cleaning, errands; all the stuff I don't do well when I am immersed in a book or movie.

She is an angel who wears many hats in my life, keeping me in a space to offer my gifts while she is a gift to me. She is often the wind beneath my wings along with my kids, my adopted parents and my adopted sis. On the level of business, she served on the board of directors for my non-profit organization in the past. She cheered me on when I was helping kids withdraw from gangs. That woman is a rock, those kids didn't scare her for a second.

I ran into a computer glitch at one o'clock Friday morning and was stopped cold from backing up my work on disk. The next day I ran into all sorts of complications attempting to work it out with "experts" that all disagreed. Later in the afternoon a friend of Costner's, who is also a friend of mine, was here to give me one of his famous deep muscle massages on my neck and back to ease the computer stress that's been kicking in. He also knew exactly how to work out my computer problem. Miracles can be unearthed in the most unlikely places.

My unexpected distractions gave me extra time to edit the work that was already done and that felt benevolent to my heart. At least I was progressing with the book. Papa Lou came Sunday to correct the glitch and I was buzzing away on the computer again like a mad woman by late afternoon.

Every writer has his or her own style for living and writing. Me, I am what could be called a marathon writer. I love to write massive amounts in spurts then rest a bit to collect myself, then start the whole process over. It is my way. Often when I am writing it is because I am inspired by an idea that I cannot shake. I jump into that idea, splash around awhile, and then dive in deep until I need a break.

I may live in my silk PJ's for days, forget to return phone calls or eat, sleep a few hours here and there, and order in food when I do remember to eat. I won't see the men in my life unless it is someone I am deeply in love with or exceptionally curious about. I am not in love right now, or exceptionally curious, so I have not dated since the book and I slipped under the sheets together.

The first one hundred and thirty pages of this book took fourteen days to write *out* including first edits. I never really know what the project will take until it is done. My best estimates are not always correct so I don't estimate much anymore. It will be done when it is done. If I must nail down a date, a by-when, I will set up some lag time, just in case I need it. The page must be given its expression. We need time to tumble around together.

I tend to be a marathon personality with other things in my life… I bite in and don't let go until my teeth get tender in my gums. I regroup and go again when I have rested a bit. I take care of myself in the best way I can when I am in the eye of the flurry. I have to get through the birthing process and see the baby born. When I am in the middle of the energy, that is all that matters. This means I have an unusual amount of failures and successes under my belt. It is a glorious way to live if you can get the gig.

As you write, it will change the way you live. If this is new to you, try on new ways of living and see what suits you. Know that you may find what fits, wear it a while, and then want to change.

For instance, I tend to be a nocturnal soul. I love the nighttime and am at my most productive between midnight and four AM. However, now that I have a massive amount of work to do during the day… the time that others are up answering their phones… I must adapt a bit. I work till about one o'clock AM and wake at nine. It is a compromise I make for my art but I miss the quiet early morning hours. Luckily, I also love the sunny California days of summer, so my complaints are minimal just now.

This morning I could not wait to get back to the computer and move forward with the book. A friend called earlier to see how things are progressing with the project. When I told her I was over half finished she was shocked. Her last book took many years to write.

"How the hell do you do it?" she asked in a perplexed manner. I sensed a touch of anger.

"I don't know. I just do it. I just listen and write what I hear."

"I am so jealous!" she said in a restless tone. "When do the workshops begin? Sign me up now, I want in!"

We laughed, but it is no laughing matter, really. It is a big problem.

Writers, like other artists, can be cruel to themselves at the level of evaluation. There is a nasty word they use that I find bitter to the taste. It is the word *should.* There is an inner dialogue that happens in their heads, a manipulative sort of chatter. The chatter says that you should be doing this and that and the other. It is truly disgusting. It keeps you separated from your own best wisdom and alters your ability to harvest a body of work to your credit.

When shoulds are used in context to my life, I say, "Stop shoulding all over me!" to the one who delivers the words then I pretend to wipe off my body like a mime would do. It is my way to release the yucky energy. We artists are not ever wise to compare ourselves to another.

Should and should've are words that act like roadblocks to writers. And they pull many a writer into writer's block unconsciously and seductively. Writer's block is a rather desolate place for most writers. It is a place brimming with lies about what is suppose to be. These lies say that there is a right and wrong way to write and a way that it should and should not look; that there is a way that a writer should and should not live and work. It is a bumfunk state of mind to dwell in… a bummer that gets you feeling funky, and not in a good way. I say watch the road signs and steer clear of writer's block.

How do you steer clear? Stop giving yourself a cluster of shoulds and start living above the influence of others who think you are not doing it… whatever it is… right. Let the judgements go that you place on yourself now. Ask the page, "What is my deepest desire in this situation?" Let it talk to you. Listen and write. Use this method of communication for any situation you encounter.

It is honestly more fun to write your life out from the page than to try to put it onto the page. To discover your life is to uncover the mysteries that were concealed or secret to you. These mysteries are your truest and most real life. When you are not sure about something, instead of asking others or relying on your logic, go to the page first. Listen. Write. Let your deep and intrinsic Extraordinary Self guide you into who you are and what you are about. Let it help you expose your own way. Be open to new avenues.

As a precious and important person, and as a rebel writer, it is crucial that you own your personality and style, and that you respect it. No one else is like you. You are a true masterpiece. Your personality will come through in your work. Let it. If you publish, it will come through to the world, so learn as much about your personality as you can. Dialogue with it and get all the clarity you need.

I recently read a book by a writer for writers. In one section especially it was obvious to me that he has a real disdain for writers who do well, have best sellers, or a natural awareness of the market that allows them to just do what they love. His fuming personality plowed through the pages like a tornado whipping through a heavy forest and splintering all the trees within its path.

"Wow," I heeded, "he's really going to hate my book!" I am doing all the things he says not to do.

But I loved his book because it was real and honest writing. His "hot button" spoke through the pages. So he has a hot button. Big deal. Perhaps some other writers might throw it across the room in anger, thrust it into the trash in passionate disobedience, or buy all the twaddle inside about how hard the writing life is and concede entirely. But I find it a wonderful expression of another writer's personal truth about his life with books.

All personal truth has value... anyone's, everyone's. So, the book, a collection of the writer's thoughts, is a treasure. I will keep it as a book to enjoy for many years to come. I will never believe that the writing life is hard for me. It is just life unfolding, neither easy nor hard. It just is. That's all. Hard? Why? Why do I need it to be nearly impenetrable? He makes it sound a bit like slavery lived within a padded cell. He is with a big house so maybe it is for him just that, a new form of slavery.

For me, the writing life is glorious. Just to be able to do the thing can put me to my knees in tears of gratitude, I don't try to pigeon hole it into one space or another. I love the complex energy about it. It suits me. If we could just learn that most of the time something that seems so laborious is happening for our highest good, we might find a little more happiness in our lives. We might live longer, be more kind to ourselves and healthier.

Sunday afternoon I did a few hours of edits and then lay down in bed to take a nap. Since I no longer have my kids home to nap with, I turned on the television for company. It can become uncomfortably quiet at my place when I am missing holding my kids. My arms ache.

C-SPAN was airing a dialogue between the traditionally published writing community and the large house publishing community. It was terribly gruesome. Everyone was attempting to be so polite and professional while the writers were clearly dying and the publishers had no solutions. The writers did not get the compassion they sought there.

The spokesperson for the publishers seemed resigned and indifferent that not anything could be done to help the writers, making the publishing system look pretty offensive on national television. Publishers want to blame the bookstores. It's all terribly messed up… everything in the industry is changing so fast nobody can think straight. The writers get the brunt of it.

I watched it to completion, closed my eyes and once again said a quiet thank you for the publisher I have.

Those big houses slay rebel writers. I am so grateful to have not gone that route of publishing and distribution. My writing life need not be a struggle like the lives of writers I heard speaking on C-SPAN. If something does not give soon, writers who sold their souls to the big houses will have to strike, protest, or something more severe to attempt to gain their souls back. Those artists were much more enraged than they were showing in front of the camera. My heart broke for them.

Every writer must find his or her own way to live and write then cherish that way. Your decisions must be made for your long-term happiness. For me, I cherish all of my life on and off the page, equitably the agonizing stuff, too. I am just so happy to be alive, writing, and making the movies that arouse my soul. The genuineness is that I am simply happy under most conditions these days. No words can describe how grateful I am to be me living my life now in this time and place. My life is a series of miracles. And that makes the whole of the world magical for me to experience.

Live and write in the way that suits and benefits you. Find your way then follow it. Don't give ear to people telling you how you *should* live or write. That's absurdity. They are not you. They cannot know what is suitable for you.

Experiment with the writing life. Make it and your writings your friends. Caress the whole of it. Frolic with it. Let your writing go wild without attempting to contain it and it will be real. Find the grace, grit, elegance, and balance residing naturally within your rebel writing spirit.

Write where you want and when you want. Find *out* what works.

Sometimes I write in my bedroom with pen and paper, propped up on the comfortable pillows I have in abundance. I write big and full like the room is. Sometimes on a huge drawing pad. My bedroom is so huge, even with its nooks and crannies that it gives me a rich feeling that comes through in writings done there. Sometimes I need the peace of the ocean to balance me when I want to indisputably write low, deep, absorbing, and rampageous from the page. I write brisk and intensely and then velvety and gradually. At times I prefer to write with music in the background, more so when I am working on a movie script, and sometimes I like to write with another writer while we both are silently writing our backbone from the page. I do what works when it works. Most of the time I am buzzing away at the computer, rarely aware of what I have written until I read it.

Occasionally a friend will read to me something I wrote years ago and I am astonished I wrote it, it seems so foreign. How profoundly I wrote, I think to myself. The page can amaze me like that. I am being given a gift, a way to see how someone else might hear my words. It is a gift without price.

Remember to let synchronicity be a messenger and a guide. Just after the C-SPAN program that reminded me how lucky I am to write as I wish, I flipped over to the Lifetime channel. I thought there would most likely be something there I could use as a lullaby. Of course, as my life goes, Lifetime chose that day and time to run Dances With Wolves… Duhhhhhh….

I rolled my eyes, let out an enormous sigh and laughed. The *Thing* had come to visit, not to my surprise. There *he* was again. Then suddenly it registered in me… the section of the film in play was the scene I mentioned earlier in my book about the trail of a true human being. These odd cosmic occurrences are so profound at times.

I got the message loud and clear and I let a wide grin grace my face and temperament. Yes, I am on that trail and life is good. I said a special little thank you to Kevin for making such a dynamic film with a story that takes my breath away and then drifted off to sleep.

Exercise: It is time to find your own way. Write down a scenario that describes your ideal life as a writer. How does this writer live and write? What is he or she like that may seem different than you? What is your internal writer's personality like? Do you like this writer you write about?

Read it over mindfully several times, adding new thoughts, as you need. Design your writing life to be what you need to experience. You can change it later, if you choose, but claim it now. Only by claiming a thing, accepting it fully, and owning your decisions can it wholly be yours.

Write anywhere. Write everywhere.
Write everything.

Wanting and Having

Our doubts are traitors, and make us lose the good we oft might win by fearing to attempt.
William Shakespeare

All people everywhere often overlook a very lucid style of living. It is based on the concept of done deals. Done deal thinking does wonders to relieve the mind of doubts and stress. I believe that writers and other artists do well to consider it, ponder it well, and take it on as part of their lifestyle. Why? It opens the doors of creativity, closes the doors of doubts, and helps you feel better all the way around. To live your life knowing that everything is already done is to live richly with true freedom.

Want is a lack-type-thinking mode. It indicates a lack of movement needed, or perceived as needed. Yet the universe is always in movement, a forward volitional thrust on your behalf. You can believe that without seeing it if you are bold enough to conceive of such a miracle. There is a downside to simple logic; it requires proof. Proof is typically the killer of miracles. As soon as you want something especially critical to your needs and believe you possibly won't get it, since you don't see it moving to you, then start to want it more, you have given birth to lack. You've chosen proof over faith and landed yourself into the grips of struggle.

Lack will take over by your silent command. Only by altering this framework with the idea and belief that you already have what you desire, watching for its manifestation through sychronicity as you are grateful, will you see the desire outpicture in your physical world.

People who want to write often don't, owing to a belief that they won't be successful in the writing world. Visions of the struggling artist abound. When in actuality, you have already arrived on the doorstep of your success, if you decide that this is true. Once you own that and claim it explicitly, the writing life will adapt itself to your dreams. And the rest of the world unconsciously follows your lead. People are typically going to believe in your dreams and support them to the extent that you do.

True determination is followed by acceptance in the outside world. That kind of determination is born of an inner acceptance, the acceptance that the thing is already done. I like to call it keeping your eye on the ball. No matter what the appearance of the world around you, remember that the outer world is like putty constantly reforming into a different mold based on your thinking, so do keep your eye on the ball at all times. Focus on the desired outcome and *know* it is done in a place beyond doubt. Forget about the naysayer's that love to steal you dreams. Don't give them the satisfaction. Be tough.

Living from a mental state of lack is true poverty. When I was a kid, maybe seven years old, my father moved us from my grandfather's farm to his second farm in a little country town in Missouri. The old two-story farmhouse had no heating except for a potbelly stove, and no running water except for a pump in the kitchen that brought up cold water from the well. There was no indoor plumbing or electricity when we arrived. This was its own form of poverty.

My sister and I took baths on Saturday afternoons in a big galvanized tub on the mud porch. My father and brother hunted and brought home squirrels and rabbits from the woods for dinner, with an occasional frog leg feast from the pond. In warmer months veggies from the garden rounded out the diet. Still, I was always near starving. When enough food was brought home, I had a horrible time eating innocent little animals. I fought every bite and often could not swallow at all.

Being near starvation was not the worst of being poor. It was actually the attitude and beliefs perpetuated within that house that hurt me in the long run. We were poor, dirt poor. Anyone could see that. My sister and I wore dresses made from flour sacks, had bowl haircuts, and one pair of shoes for the whole year. If our feet grew and our toes curled in… oh well, we lived with it. I could survive being hungry and cold for a few years until things changed, but fighting the spoon-fed belief in lack took almost another thirty years to break free from. It loomed over me like a dark penetrating cloud.

Feeling poor makes you sick inside and eventually hurts your body. Getting past the idea that I would always be poor and hungry, that it was a curse, was like scratching my way out of a deep dark hole that you have been buried in alive by mistake. It makes you terrified of life, timid and weak. The belief that you could never win is hard to live with. We all need to win.

Today I know that lack is a lie. How I survived its clutch is a miracle. I simply stopped believing in the lie. I started to know that my needs are met in a place I cannot see, and I expect them to be resolved in the physical reality. I accepted abundance and abundance said, "It is good to see you come home."

As a single mom raising two kids for most of their lives, I've had my tight times, but it has been many years since I was poor in spirit. Even when I was flat broke and seemingly busted, I knew I was rich inside where it mattered most, so conditions shifted as I expected. I learned that taking outer conditions too seriously is not wise.

Rebel writers can address lack and find out what it is trying to tell them. It is a teacher, like any other element of life. Here is a piece from my pages written during a tight period when businesses in Scottsdale, Arizona, became unusually slow during a massive heat wave. It was the height of summer, 120 in the shade. People did not go out unless they absolutely had to. My business was dead. I'd gone to the page for comfort and reassurance.

Lee: You have not won, you know. You never really win.

Lack: Maybe. But I am leading the dance right now. I am in charge. Your electricity is in danger of being shut off and your phone bill is due. You barely have food money for the kids. What will you eat?

Lee: You're trying to scare me. It's not that serious.

Lack: How did you get yourself in this mess?

Lee: Temporary insanity... I believed in you for moments of my childhood and I've spent most of my adult life paying for that belief. You are evil, an evil lie living in the minds of millions and perpetuated by society. But I don't believe in you anymore. I don't believe in evil. What is it exactly that you are trying to communicate to me with your presence?

Lack: Isn't it obvious? I am a lie and you can do better. I can be harsh, yes... but if you see me as a lie, you can overcome me. If you win, I will just find some other innocent child to haunt. I won't miss you. I do what I have to do to get your attention, that's all.

Lee: Why did you visit our family to begin with?

Lack: I was invited. I mean, these were not the brightest people in the world, you know. Country bumpkins and all that.

Lee: Yes, I can see that now. That's how you would see it with your limited scope. You are not so smart yourself. It does not take smarts to prey on the weak. I suppose I should thank you for the lesson. I have been made stronger and wiser by the deep desire to overcome you. It is true, only the strong can be kind and the weak must be cruel. You are weak and cruel! There is no room for you in my spirit or my house. The bills are paid in a place I cannot see with my human eye, but I see it with my spirit. I have the money now. The kids and I are taken care of. God is taking care of us.

Lack: Oh, God again... God annoys me. Totality messes with my fun. Gets in the way.

Lee: Yeah, well, you're history, Bub! I am not a starving little girl anymore. I don't cry from the winter's cold and I will never have to live like that again. With God as my witness, I will never be hungry or cold again! I am not poor. I am not poor!

You are poor. You are sick. And you are weak. You prey on the innocent. How sick is that!

Lack: Gutsy, aren't you? There was a time when I could scare you into sheer panic by just showing up.

Lee: Yes. And you will never grab my spirit again. It is surrounded with light and protected by my angels.

Lack: They are a hardy bunch, those angels. I will give them that. And that Jesus character who hangs around keeping his eye on the sparrow... what a character! Oh, all this miracle stuff bores me to tears. Blah, blah, blah! Yawn... yawn... I'm gonna fly... you bore me. It is only fun when I can mess with your head.

Lee: Good! Then I have succeeded.

Lack: You win this round Red, I gotta fly. Things to do, people to scare.

My bills were paid the next day when a client owing me money paid her rather large debt. Two days later my office was flooded with clients responding to the depressed heat conditions with agitation. This was no coincidence. I dialogued many times with lack until I became so boring that lack stopped showing up in the page. That's when you know you've cleared a pocket of energy. Facing a fear like lack and less gives you power over your life. When you feel stronger, you are stronger. It is easier to be assertive from a position of power.

When you desperately want something, it means you probably don't believe you have it in the unseen. Until you see it done there first, you will be operating from lack.

Want and desire are different energies. To desire something, knowing that it is done, usually means that your spirit is growing bigger and you are willing to accept more. This is sometimes known as divine discontent; a good thing for our soul's development, while wanting, by its very nature, will keep you distant from your manifestation. What you fear the most, not having, comes upon you. Claiming a thing as done is one of the most authoritative choices we can make to be accountable for our lives.

If you believe that the writer in you is alive, awake, and well… then it is so. It is done. I suggest you go to the page and meet that writer each day, even if it is just fifteen minutes, and remind this part of you that it is okay to write. Furthermore, it's okay to write poorly just to get the ball rolling. Be a loving and caring coach and teacher. Free it. Tell it about done deals. Tell it that you will go to the page and meet it there regularly. Make that promise and keep it.

All things in heaven and earth are already done. Everything. Accept your life as it is and then find ways to expand it by expanding your belief system to include done deals. Such a choice will reduce your stress levels immensely.

My childhood seems like it happened lifetimes ago now. That little girl who suffered long and so oppressively is elegant and progressive now… one hell of a woman, drastically different from her beginnings. Life is great when you can get a kick out of yourself and you're the only one laughing.

Poverty, the living and thinking of it, is not a great gift to give a kid. But the universe, in its wisdom, knew how to turn my life around. It was in my plan to be a survivor and a warrior. There is no one to blame for my suffering. I clearly chose it.

The fact that you are reading this book potentially means that it is in your plan to get the messages in these pages for your own growth. We all have a past and no matter what it was like, loving it will help transcend it.

Lack hates to be loved in the beginning; it is such an intense brat child. It kicks and screams and has a fit. But if you just continue to love it in spite of its ugliness, it gives up and moves on or becomes a friendly teacher. To love the unlovable is a grand achievement that changes things inside and outside of us.

In the end, the thing that heals everything in life, your life and the lives of others, is love and acceptance. Accepting that you have *without seeing it* will cure you of wanting. Love want for the lessons that it gives you and then thank it and let it go.

Conjure up the writer from the bottom of your soul... give it breath and meaning, give it life and room to grow. Love and accept the writer in you to expression. It does not matter if you write for yourself or for the world; it is all the same. *You are a writer.* The part of you that writes is a life long friend and treasure. Choose well what and who you love and you will be made more well by your accountable choices.

When something in your life is not seemingly working and you have accepted it as a done deal, it just means a timing issue is afoot. Within your plan is perfect order. Trust that. When you originated this plan before bombing in here, you operated in a state of pure genius. Nothing existed to dilute it. Your plan is inherently perfect, as you are perfect within your imperfections.

Evenhandedly continue to claim what is done at that other level and relax as you watch for signs. You will always receive little reminder signs to let you know the universe is at work on your behalf. It is all part of the done deal in motion, the obvious mystery of the universal breadcrumb trail. Follow your instincts, they are stronger and wiser than your logic, which likes to entertain doubt.

When my fears and I meet on an even playing field, we can become the greatest of friends. The game will be over when it is no longer necessary.

Personal Notes:

Cherish the Process

Dear love, be not impatient with the world, but value its intricate structure. It is the putty we use to shape your dreams into being by your own hand.

When it seems that nothing is happening "out there", everything is happening... and like the earth spinning on its axis, you cannot see the progress with your naked eye. Therefore, go within where it is easier to see the done deal completed. Know that all is well and miracles are the very ground you walk upon. If doubt appears, learn what its message is. Accept the message and tell it that you love it for the lesson, but today, you choose not to play. Let it go.

Always choose your master wisely, either faith or doubt. Both serve in their own ways as teachers, but doubt makes the lessons more laborsome. Doubt believes in struggling.

Be bold and harness the whole of the universe... say yes to all that you desire and it is done unto you. Want not, for it is a thief. Be patient in the quiet times. Do what you are guided to do and be the best of yourself for this will bring you happiness.

So relax. Pet a puppy, watch an infant sleep, and write love letters to your enemies. Life is yours to cherish dear love. It is a magical moment in the eye of infinity... a mere speck... but a speck of grand importance.

Taken from The Angel Pages

Writing is a process much like pregnancy. For men, it is a way to experience birth without morning sickness, to have the baby grow inside and taste the indefinable excitement of expectancy. Since writing is based on ideas, thoughts, and concepts, we give birth as we write the words out onto the page. Each letter is a cell of a child being born.

Ideas require a gestation period, like children require in womb. The augmentation to your spirit is a momentous occasion happening where you can't see it, but clearly happening. The baby will be born. What will it look like? You will know when you see it. But like every human child, you can count on the fact that it will be a unique masterpiece… a one of a kind creation.

Rebel writers digest this awareness and can be patient and flexible with their work when it requires time to evolve. When a *downtime* hits, just continue to casually dialogue on the page with the writer in you, or write out your thoughts and feelings to the worker of miracles inside, as if it were a person.

Once just after a one week downtime, I wrote a script for a film in four days. People marveled at my genius. I had to laugh quietly. What they refused to understand was that the baby had been growing for years, maybe eons. It was ready to deliver. I sensed its presence during the downtime just prior to birth. Two months later I wrote another script, a more elaborate piece, in one week. Again they marveled - and so did I!

I had no previous conscious association with the piece. It was just waiting in the page like a hitchhiker, waiting for the next adventuresome writer to come along and stop. And I had stopped, became attracted and opened the door. I let the story in.

It was that story's time to be born and it turned into an absolutely beautiful film. A student filmmaker at UCLA took it on when I was twenty. I had an acting role and a ton of fun learning about filmmaking. But I have not seen or heard from the filmmaker since.

My job was just to write *out* the story and give it life on the page. Then my end of the work was done. The hitchhiker and I parted ways on friendly terms.

We naturally retain internal access to millions of stories, more than we could ever write in one lifetime. They float in and around us all day long. Still, there are important downtimes when you just need to rest and take care of yourself, do dumb things and get wildly sidetracked. Withdraw to Mexico for a few days or look in on the redwoods... whatever. Do what is around you that won't strain you mentally or emotionally. Be relaxed in whatever you do and don't make a fuss over anything.

When a downtime hits, I like to do a lot of nothing since I am otherwise in marathon mode and accomplishing more than even I can grasp. This creates a nice sense of balance that feels peaceful and secure. I am just "hanging out" with friends or myself. Just being. I am usually still writing, but it is casual. I am most composed when I write everyday, even if it is simply to journal.

I may hang out in bed for a couple of days and read, nap, or watch a bunch of movies that I have not gotten to see as long as I was in marathon mode. I may converse with friends that thought I dropped off the planet, or attend private screenings with actor or director friends who I have not seen in a long stretch. Maybe I will pray more than usual. Or just do nothing at all except lie in the sun and sleep. I might just stare at the ocean and thank God for the music it makes.

Cherish the gestation times for what they are, a time leading to childbearing. The baby is fine. It is a bit like birthing a new relationship. When you first get into it, you are knocking around, finding your footing, perceiving what is there. You are wise not to hold any grand expectations since you don't know what you're dealing with yet. In this new environment you are a tourist. The mood is festive because you are casually exploring.

For me, writing is always a pleasant activity, probably in light of my attitude about it. I am just listening to the page. I am not working at it, even when I am writing my insides out of the page and they are old and ugly and loaded with painful memories. Often I have no idea what I will write until I come to the page; I can't mentally compose the elements of a universe so measureless and endless. I put my cup under the spout, so to speak, and it is filled each and every time. I expect that to happen. I have a sincerely ostentatious cup.

When I am not in marathon mode, I date more often. I am extremely choosy and will frequently be drawn to certain men during downtimes that represent comfort to me.

I dated a wonderful actor for a while who called himself my "sanctuary" and he surely was, especially during a downtime. I loved those times when I saw more of him because it was always extremely easy to simply be alive in his presence. We both felt relaxed and centered, so very elated to cut out time together. Our schedules did not allow for this to happen often so when we did get an open door, it led to great bouts of goofiness and making love; a combination of energy that I truthfully cherish. His acting abilities make him an unpredictable comedian and I loved that.

He's the guy each and every woman wishes they had in their lives. The one who gives you a little gift as soon as you arrive and then throws rose petals over you as you are leaving. I knew what I had, how precious and wonderful it was to see him and what a gift he was to me. I respect the time for what it was... pure magic.

Magic exists in quiet moments and in all other moments. Use your downtimes, times of less activity, to pamper yourself with gifts and treasures. Go at your own pace and just regroup and reenergize your mind, heart, body, and soul. Be good to yourself. Keep your eyes open for unexpected synchronicities, too.

Exercise: Take a downtime of one to two days and see what you feel at the end of it. Dialogue with the writer in you to get a scope on what was happening beyond your visual physical sight. The writer may have his or her own experience separate from yours. The writer is always writing, even when you are doing other things. The writer is always pregnant with possibilities.

"I can see you. Can you see me?
I am 'the writer within'.
Set me free!"

Personal Notes:

Personal Notes:

Writers and Relationships

You have to know what you want to get. But when you know that, let it take you. And if it seems to take you off the track, don't hold back, because perhaps that is instinctively where you want to be. And if you hold back and try to be always where you have been before, you will go dry.

Gertrude Stein

The more rebel writing you do the more important solid and valuable relations with other writers will become. In fact, all of your relationship may change right before your eyes as you change.

There are a few things worth mentioning here in regards to the subject of relationships that may save you some time, trouble, and grief. Ponder them.

Crazymakers are the people who are so totally unpredictable that they drive you nuts and must be avoided completely, no matter how seductive they are. These are the people who are unable to care enough about their own well being to honor yours. Subtle control and suppression is their game. The first time you feel that you must make an excuse for someone in your life, you have reasonably encountered a crazymaker. Run away; don't walk. But leave this person to his or her own devices.

This may sound harsh, it may be harsh, but crazymakers demand to be dealt with in a straightforward and stern manner. They are users, and if they are in your life, you are being used. This will affect your happiness and your writing in the long run. A crazymaker is an unstable personality, unable to respect others, including you. *You* get no special graces here... no one ever does with them.

In regards to sharing your work with others, there are special considerations. Treat your work, as it is, a gift to you and to the world. And don't throw pearls before swine. Remember that your writing is your infant child. You wouldn't place your own child in harms way, so take heed. Again, this appears harsh. It is. I have seen many a writer broken into emotionally fragmented minute pieces by some mediocre-minded dunderhead with no heart that ripped a priceless piece asunder in front of the unprepared writer.

Hold your work as sacred and share it with only people that have earned your trust. When what others say is of no importance to you, you can be better prepared to put it out there to strangers. Until then, lay low. Take care of your baby.

Anyone who wants to deconstruct your work is to be avoided. The only kind of stimulus you need, especially if you are new to this writing life, is the kind that highlights all the great chunks in your work. You need positive affirmations, not criticism. All the kinks will work themselves out if the "good" stuff is recognized and applauded.

Remember that your work is a living organism. It is not just words on paper. It has a full and rich life. In the page yet unwritten is another life. And another, and on and on. You will never run out of ideas. If an idea hits and you are not in a position to catch it, don't dwell on it. Other ideas and thoughts will present themselves as you listen to the page.

And last but not least, please treasure yourself enough to keep a distance from authors who believe they have some special talent (that you don't have) just because they have been published. If you choose to have a writing partner or two, make certain there is no hidden ego agenda going on. That agenda will suck you dry and make you feel small, which you aren't.

No one on this planet is better than you or lesser than you. Those who play that game are users in their own ways that are difficult to detect. Again, run away; don't walk away. When the time comes that you are fully accepting of yourself as a wonderful writer, you can casually saunter along and not be disturbed by the foolishness of others.

Why do I say these things… when every bit of this chapter seems harsh? I do so to make a point. You are worth the best in all areas of your life. These are not just words. At some point we must all live this truth.

There are people in this world who harbor hidden jealousy about writers, musicians, actors… any artist, just about anyone who does what they love with their life. If they are successful, they get a double hit. These antagonists are not bad people, they are just excessively insecure. But that insecurity *will* rub off on you if you get too close to it for too long. Users come with a price and it typically is not worth paying.

Personal Notes:

Stewardship: Rebels Who Publish

The greater the contrast, the greater the potential. Great energy comes from a correspondingly great tension between opposites.

C G Jung

Rebel writers bring to light penetrating truths. They are stewards in their own right. Look at any noteworthy piece of work and you will find a rebel hidden between the lines. They route advancements in thinking and activity. They see a problem or a potential problem and speak out toward a greater reality. Without rebels our society would be colorless, monotone, and dispassionate.

I tend to do well with complex individuals that wear their rebel spirits on their sleeves, as well as those that are not so obvious about it. Either way, I am inspired. It is why I harmonize beautifully into the writing world, the filmmaking world, and can live comfortably in Hollywood with its inherent crudeness. In all these arenas rebels are blasting off into new directions.

For rebel writers who plan to publish, I would remind you of this one important note: Don't shelter your life or words unless you absolutely must. You typically do not gain anything worth having when playing life safe, oppressively, and overly structured. Declare what you need to say and continue to catapult your thoughts forward. A wet towel over burning words is a sad thing when the words need be stated. There is an emotional price to pay for the choice of suppression, one that is hard to live with. You cheat the world and yourself. It is an act of personal dishonor. And your point won't get heard; your work won't make a difference in the world.

A man I know has had a couple of talks with Shirley MacLaine. We talked recently about her books. I remember what it was like when she began to put her straightforward voice into print. What an uproar! The press went on a rampage. My friend was saying what a wonderful person Shirley is, and after seeing her contributions, I believe him. She opened the door for others and that is a profound thing that is so magnificently wise it is difficult to consider with our limited minds. She took a momentous risk and I praise her for that.

Something ancient and cavernous inside me rocks and shakes, trembles and howls and cries torrents of rapture when a rebel steps forward in print or film. I live for those moments! Every cell in my body screams, "Go! Go!" My heart pumps like the heart of an animal that's been perused at the tip of a spear and has outrun the hunter.

There's a crisp and lightening-like alchemy alive in a person who storms the Bastille of consciousness and roars like a lion into the numbness, shattering the glass walls of common thought. It sweeps me away. My own passions are set loose to auto-jet freely into the world of thought and possibility.

I am aware that the crux of my passion is a bottomless, devoted, sanctifying, defiant, and unspeakable love. As Plato said, "Love has made men and women dare to die for their beloved." When that crispness snaps and sparks within me, I feel the passion I have for all people known and unknown.

I believe that rebels write and act from love for the whole, even if they are not aware of their truest intent.

And if there were only some way of contriving that a state or an army should be made up of lovers and their loves, they would be the very best governors of their own city, abstaining from all dishonour, and emulating one another in honour; and when fighting at each other's side, although a mere handful, they would overcome the world.

Plato

I am a rebel who publishes. I must. I am driven to do so. My love for this world and the people in it must be expressed in the most creative deportment possible. It is explicitly how I must live to feel that I am honoring myself. No one else need understand; it is between my God and me. And so others do understand.

If you choose to publish, know why you are doing it. If it is to receive fame and notoriety, that's not enough. Fame can leave you feeling empty if you weren't brimming to begin with. Know why because you are worth knowing that about yourself. Go to the page and ask it why you are publishing before you commit. It will tell you everything you are willing to hear.

Shirley MacLaine had fame, money, and success. She did not need to gain more of the same through her books. So we have gained, all of us.

I say thanks, Shirley.

Personal Notes:

Raw Writing and Miss Lindsay Spann

When her words go onto this page they become immortal. Her thoughts are recorded for all time and space and ripple into the universe, returning to earth as light in the darkness. These words, to the thinking man and woman, are sacred. All awareness shared is not just her gift, but God's. No writer is without guidance. No writer is without meaning. No writer is without the steady hand of creation gently caressing the heart of the instrument. This young one's voice is not without purpose and plan. It is with gratitude that we say this.

Taken from The Angel Pages

Last night I couldn't sleep. Excitement kept my mind busy and my heart receptive and stirred by the night's thoughts. I will be sharing a gift with you today, one that was shared with me. This absolutely thrills me!

This morning I rushed to the computer to set about these words onto the turbulent sea of mankind. And now I can relax and be with the page. Here I find peace in the midst of hopefully rocking *your* world with this chapter.

I sit before the page in my home office that overlooks the comforting courtyard of plants and water resting peacefully outside my windows as if waiting there for my enjoyment. I am gazing off to my right and into the eyes of Miss Lindsay Spann from a photo printed in the LA Times. There is an aliveness and grace in those bold, yet, soft eyes that moves me… this young woman has profound significance in the world. She is a wake up call to the whole of society.

She may not have intended it that way… maybe she was simply telling her truth, but it is a reverberating truth that can change things, us, for the better.

Lindsay is a teenage writer with an ocean-like soul, a weighty plethora of wisdom to express, and the faculty of listening to the page to support her.

My assistant and friend, Irene Park, who saw Lindsay's essay entitled *Listen to Your Children* in the Times after the shootings at Columbine High School, brought her work to my attention. The moment I read it I knew I needed to place it in my book as a clear example of raw rebel writing.

As I have said, such writing smears truth in our faces. It is not always pretty and fluffy like a newborn kitten… it is more like a landslide from a rain soaked hill crashing down on our heads. One we can walk away from and the other we must deal with. The landslide can pull people together and make them work toward a common goal. The kitten is simply sweet and cute; it is no call to change.

You will read in this chapter a call to greater understanding, a shout for change and action. Lindsay speaks for a generation bellowing from the page in a place we can't see, but she can hear. If we heed the outcry, put our magisterial egos to one side, we can understand something about the secret world of kids and why kids are killing kids these days with semiautomatic weapons instead of just punching each other in the nose.

The race was on to find Lindsay Spann as soon as I finished reading her essay. Between Irene and myself, it took a few phone calls and some detective work, and was well worth the effort.

When I spoke to Lindsay and her mother, it was a distinguished moment. Lindsay's voice is so soft over the phone, barely above a whisper. On paper it roars and blazes and rumbles. This is a girl who knows how to get heard and we will do well to listen.

Lindsay wanted to talk to me first and had several well-thought-out questions. She also wanted to say thanks for the opportunity she was being given to have her work seen and distributed across the globe. It was hard for me to tell her that it is she who deserves the thanks. I was fighting off tears then as I am now. I *get* this young woman's voice. It is hitting like a cannon shot into my soul.

There is much I could say about Lindsay, but she speaks well for herself from the page. I think you will see that. I am including two of her pieces that you will get a full picture of the vast reservoirs of talent that opens her to the page. She offers truth commonly hidden behind our fears and mechanical defenses.

What follows is the essay that shook my bones and led me to comprehend that this Miss Lindsay Spann is a powerhouse. Exactly the kind of writer I love to read. She is raw… undiluted… staggering. I am grateful that our paths have crossed.

<u>**Listen to Your Children**</u>

Lindsay Spann

Shut up. Turn off the TV. Put down the newspaper. Stop drinking your Scotch. Stop taking your Prozac. Put away your to-do list. Turn off your aromatherapy. Put away your cell phone. Turn off your pager, fax and computer. Stop your four-wheel-drive vehicle and refrain from looking in the rearview mirror at your graying, balding hair and crow's-feet wrinkles.

Look at us instead, your children.

Look past our tattoos, our pierced body parts, naked abdomens and colored, spiked hair. Those are the subtle attention-getters before guns and school massacres. After all, wasn't that what you said to your parents, with your long hair, peace beads, Woodstock and "peace, love and happiness"? You are listening to us about as much as your parents listened to you. It feels to us the same way it did to you. Bad. It feels bad.

Remember how your parents blamed and pointed their fingers at everyone but themselves? They preached lack of morals. Blamed drugs, the pill, the black movement, women's lib. Déjà vu? Well, you learned really well how to avoid doing the hardest work required of humans: listening to another perspective, understanding, looking for commonality and then taking the time to build the bridge of acceptance. When you don't like the rules or the laws, you just change them to suit your needs of the day. Who cares about the consequences on the past or future generations? That's the power of numbers – baby boomer numbers.

It seems implausible to you that any other generation could have another point of view. We are obliterated in the huge shadow of your presence. You twist and change meanings of words and ways of thinking, no matter how illogical, to suit your needs, blame others, manipulate for profit and shun responsibility.

But we see right through your hypocrisy. We know about your "recreational drugs" of the 60's, rationalized as mind-expanding and consciousness-raising. They later turned into your drug habit demons, along with group therapy, 12 step programs and detox centers. We scoff at your pathetic "just say no" slogan, as if it worked for you. Get real.

Remember self-actualization and how it quickly turned into the "me generation" and instant gratification with junk bonds, savings and loan failures and credit card debts?

Now you tell us to save while you spend all of your own resources and that of our grandparents. You tell us to care for the environment that you ransacked and obliterated by your quest for better and best. You preach simplicity after you burp, then pat your paunchy, satisfied belly. You tell us to abstain from sex for fear of HIV or other sexually transmitted diseases while you scan the Internet for private porn sites and sex chat rooms. You cheat on your marriage vows, have affairs, and don't call sex sex. Do you think we don't know that what you preach to us doesn't match your actions? And we have to love and depend on you anyway.

You still want your cake and to eat it too, don't you? You never want to ante up and pay for your choices or clean up your messes. You just move to a clean spot. Now you just want to change the rules. Well, lots of those rules are not man-made, so you can't change them. So, eventually, you are going to die, and we inherit the mess, without a clue as to how to clean it up. Because you never taught us how.

Save your children. Build the bridges. Listen. Slow down. Take the time.

We, your kids, shouldn't have to commit suicide or kill each other to get your attention.

When will we listen? When will be put our desires and perceived needs aside and take care of our children? When will we respect that they need us desperately and will do just about anything to be seen and heard? When will we understand their value and magnificence?

This piece hit me for personal and obvious reasons. I am enamored with kids. They are God's greatest miracles. And I believe they are the most disrespected arms of society. Their voices are often ignored… we foolishly believe that age has something to do with intelligence. We could not be more wrong, dead wrong. The Littleton shootings proved that.

The two boys who murdered a teacher and twelve classmates were no dummies. They were intensely underestimated; a mistake too often made with kids. And I suspect that they were ignored too often. How can your child be building bombs in your garage without your knowledge unless you've been far too distracted? It does not take a rocket scientist to figure this one out.

Raising my own two kids, Patrick Charles and Kate, by myself, involved choices I made after much prayer. I am accountable for the choice to divorce their alcoholic father and try to save the kids and myself from living in danger. History had repeated itself. I had put myself in a situation with another rageaholic and had to fight my way to freedom.

P.C. was with me only in small portions of time and Kate was with me full-time until she moved out onto her own. During the years they needed me I set aside my writing and film career. I wrote but did not pursue publication with any solid intent. I produced and hosted radio and television shows to help pay the bills but decreased those activities when fame began to lessen our privacy. I disappeared from the limelight to maintain a strong presence at home.

Kate is my youngest. When she went out on her own, so did I.

Am I behind in my career? Yes… maybe. Actually, there is no way to know that. But I am a mom first, a better than average mom according to my kids, and that is a good thing to live with when I lay my head down at night. When they needed me I was there for them. Even when they did not *need* my direct attention and wanted to spread their wings a bit, hugs, kisses, encouragement, smiles, love notes, naps together, daydreaming, a non-critical ear to bend and silliness were available at a moments notice. My house was so popular that all the kids in the neighborhood wanted to move in!

I admit that it was emotionally difficult and taxing at times. I felt my wings wanting to spread out into other directions, too. But I kept my eye on the ball. I knew my time would come. And it has.

My kids are what the world would label "good and well-mannered kids" who just happen to have a lot of me in them. It will be interesting to see what their contributions to the world will be.

Two things will stick in my mind forever. The first is the way my daughter made sure to tell me daily how she loves me, and how happy she is that I am *her* mom. She tells me that she is the lucky one. More tears are rolling as I write this… I would have died to be able to say those things to either of my parents, or to kiss them and hug them the way Kate does me almost every time she passes through a room that I am in. I would have loved for my friends to say, "Man, your mom is the coolest!" the way my kid's friends do.

The second is the way my son fathers his little girl. A kid who had absolutely no effective examples of fatherhood broke the mold. If he never succeeds beyond this contribution, the angels will sing far and wide into the heavens.

I am more proud of him than I have words for. I was hesitant when he and his wife wanted to have a child so early in their lives, but now when I see him hold sweet little Shyliina, it moves me deeply. She knows beyond a doubt that her daddy loves and cherishes her.

As P.C. says of his life with his wife and child, "Mom, I hit the jackpot! I am the luckiest man in the world!"

I have been given an awesome gift. My little boy has become the man I wished my own father could have been. He understands the magnificent opportunity he has been given. This is very rare.

All these insights and memories were invoked by the discovery of Lindsay's work.

The beauty of reading rebel writing, raw and undiluted writing, is that you can let it take you to another time and place. When you return to now, you appreciate your life even more.

Lindsay's second piece will help you further understand the presence of her voice. She has been endowed with a talent for hearing the page loud and clear, and her heart the same way. For reasons that I do not understand, God finds his greatest instruments in those of us who are different from the norm.

The following piece will give you insight into Lindsay's personal life. You may find she speaks for you, too, even though you may appear to be worlds apart. That separation is an illusion. This piece was written for LA Youth, a citywide newspaper for and by teenagers.

'I Wish You Could See Me for Who I Am'

Lindsay Spann

I am the kid you think is a loner. Not quite a geek, but definitely not popular. Sometimes, I actually feel invisible when you talk about the sleepover parties you had that I wasn't invited to or when you talk about the movies you saw. Sometimes I wonder if you are laughing at me when I see you giggling. I just look away like I don't see you or I don't care. But inside I wish for that easy way of being it looks like you have. I wonder what it would be like to have someone spend time with me because they are interested in my opinions, my humor, my caring. I see movies and read books about teenagers who are nothing like me. I feel alien or that I was born at the wrong time, or at times I shouldn't be born at all.

I'm a special-needs kid, a disabled kid. I have hemaplegia, a paralysis or inability to move certain muscles – my right side in my case. This paralysis makes it hard for me to speak above a loud whisper. I also have cataracts, so I can't see very well. I'm not cramped up like a pretzel and I don't drool out the side of my mouth or have seizures like the other kids who have the same label.

But I have difficulties on the inside that you can't see. I'm slower because I have to figure out a way to get things done that are usually easy. I work real hard every day at things that come easy to you: walking up and down the stairs, running, seeing my schoolwork or speaking up for myself. What takes you one step takes me six.

I wish that you could just see me for who I am. I wish you could include me in your conversations. I wish I could tell you about my cats or my dog and rabbit.

My first two pets were cats: Sunny and Rosco. They were great cats. Sunny loved to jump up on a high bar in the living room and view everything below. Rosco was the dignified queen who often sat outside "guarding" our house. One year, Rosco ran away. After putting up signs, walking the neighborhood, and putting ads in the local newspapers, I thought she was gone forever. Then a week later, though we had scoured every hiding place in the house at least 20 times, she came walking down our white carpet stairs, acting like a debutante at her coming-out party. Both cats died when they were 13. Sunny had to be put to sleep because she had seizures and Rosco died of an illness. It was a difficult year for me, losing my two best friends. Before they died, a stray cat showed up at my family's garage sale one Saturday. She was the dirtiest cat I had ever met, with the loudest meows. We named her Feather. She was blue-eyed, deaf and a bit stupid, but her loving nature made up for everything. Feather also got sick and had to be put to sleep on the day after my 13th birthday.

My Dad tried to soften the loss by getting me a gray rabbit named Thumper. He didn't like her because she bit and scratched him and chewed on his carpet and telephone wires. However, she was always gentle and sweet to me. She also died when I was 13.

With the passing of my pets, I ached inside. I hadn't made any human best friends at my new school, New Roads. My aunt took me to the animal shelter and I picked out a new orange-and-white cat. In honor of my previous cat, her name is Feather also. She is still alive and gives me lots of pleasure and love. My aunt also gave me her German Shepherd, Angel. He stays at her house, but I get to train him, wash and walk him and most important, love him. His is sweet and docile until a stranger passes by. Then he barks loudly and places himself between others and me to protect me.

I also have a dog-walking business called PAWS. I have walked four dogs: Timmy, Beau, Luna and Bo. All these animals are my best friends. When I talk to them, they listen and keep my conversations private. They don't know I'm disabled. They treat me the same as they treat everyone else.

Since I was seven, I have done a sport called "horse vaulting." I have learned to do amazing things: I can stand, do somersaults and perform other tricks on the horse. It's given me a lot of confidence. Every year I participate in a solo performance on "Fun Day." One year, Nancy and President Ronald Reagan gave me a medal. What a thrill!

But, I am lonely for a human friend, a best friend. My sister has friends; at the dinner table, she talks about them. My mother has friends, too. Is it my disabilities that people just don't know how to deal with? Or is it my shyness or how I look or how I act?

If I had a best friend, we could do so much together – laugh at jokes, talk about dogs, write notes to each other, share secrets, listen to each other and cheer each other on when we accomplish something great. She would never worry what people thought of her. She'd be adventuresome, strong and honest – she wouldn't be afraid to tell me what I might not like to hear.

I would like to have a best friend but if I could not, I would like to be included more often. Would you include me if I were any different? If I ran for student council would you include me? What would it take for a special needs kid to be liked? Does anyone know how lonely it is or how much work it is for me to belong to a "normal" world? I wish there was some large print instruction manual to tell me how I can belong, too.

Having been a kid who did not fit and often felt invisible, I relate to Lindsay. The friend she longs for is a friend I also longed for and eventually became to others.

As an adult, I often meet other adults who feel the same as Lindsay, though they do not have her disabilities. They have other disabilities that cannot be seen with the naked eye, like self-loathing or severe insecurities. It makes me wonder… we all have some kind of issue, so why treat Lindsay or anyone else as if they are different from ourselves?

Our society is not kind to those who are different… those who break the cookie cutter mold. Maybe Lindsay's essay can help us see that we all pay a price for such narrow-mindedness. In truth, were we brave enough to admit it, Lindsay is the kind of friend we all seek. Someone authentic and real. It just takes one step forward to look past the disability (which is really our problem) and be home free.

These essays, both published in the Times, have brought in a flood of mail for Lindsay, some kind and not so kind. Those who write raw from the page are bolder than most and as Einstein said, "Great spirits will always encounter violent opposition from mediocre minds."

I don't know where this priceless gift and magnificent young woman are bound, but I pray that her voice will continue to act as a wake up call to all. Wherever it is that she is destined, it is a very special mission she is held by.

Lindsay has the capacity to hear the page and find within it her lost and hidden parts. She has opened that door to her Extraordinary Self. If we would all go to the page to meet these parts and give them life, they would heal us. Our parts can help us remember that we are powerful and worthwhile.

I disagree with writers who say that writing is not a healer, that it is just a thing we do. It can never be *just* a thing we do, it is an extension of the natural depth within us that makes us whole and affirmed and that is a step to wellness.

Any time we use the words "just" and "only" to describe a thing or person we have gone to the shallow end of the pool. We discount that which we label this way.

It's like walking into a restaurant alone, feeling on top of the world and ready to eat a horse, then the hostess says, "Just you?" That "just" is cutting. You know what I am talking about.

Lindsay is not just another kid with disabilities. She is a challenge, a voice ringing in our ears. Are you brave enough to *hear* her? To learn from her? To be her friend? Let's not overlook what we've read in this chapter. Let's, instead, use it to heal.

The next time you see a disabled person, ask yourself if you can really continue to turn away. In that person is Lindsay Spann, an angel who looks incredibly human.

Be not forgetful to entertain strangers, for thereby some have entertained angels unawares.

Hebrews 13:2

Harmony is the reconciliation, not of opposite elements, but of elements which disagreed once,
and are now harmonized.

Plato

Personal Notes:

Lovers

Love is the eldest of the gods, and the source of the greatest good. For an honorable love is the best incentive to virtue.
Plato

I suspect that when I am old, crumpled and white-haired, I will still believe that all sensible and insightful people are better off in the company of a compassionate lover. Okay, yes… yes… it is a bit old-fashioned and I know that, but I cannot deny what my second sight tells me. At least, for me, I am a much-preferred person to be around if I am in love with a wonderful man.

This can present a bit of a conflict since I am clearly picky and I don't jump into a relationship quickly when I do encounter a man I am interested in. I don't do high dives into black bottom pools. And I don't say the words "I love you" loosely. If I say the words I expect to do the thing. You see my rather awkward dilemma. Still, I do encourage writers, especially rebel writers, to love and love well a significant other.

If you are glorified enough to have a love in your life at this time, I have some ideas for you to play with.

Write love letters to your lover and do it often. There is magic in this process. Love will speak from the page its truth. If you are at work, fax a love note in the middle of the day to your beloved. If you go to lunch together or have an afternoon rendezvous, slip a delicious love letter in a pocket ever so secretly. Let your lover find it later when he or she is not expecting to uncover the treasure.

I've had some wonderful moments with the men in my life that loved my passions… passions that are barely controllable. I love being in love once I get there. It makes the whole world brim with enchantment.

Here is a love letter slipped into the sock of a sweet man I am blessed to have shared company with. When he found this letter… well, the one shot back to me was the most ravishing thing I have ever read. I thought the paper would scorch my fingers! Sorry, I can't share it here. He felt it would lose something in print as he considers it sacred. He's right. I share mine to him that you will consider writing your own.

Thursday, 2:13 AM

I am propped on pillows here beside you watching you sleep. It's like a habit that has kidnapped my will. I am looking at your hand... such a magnificent creation resting on my leg. Calm. Anchoring me to you. You put it there while sound asleep, the way you kiss me in the night and have no memory of it. And the way you snuggle into me with each move I make. God, I love that so. We move well together. I love sleeping so close to you.

My Lord, how can I tell you how beautiful you are just now? How will you ever believe my words? Could you provide me such mercy?

I wonder how you walk around all day looking like this and not wanting to stare into mirrors. If I were so beautiful as you, I'd be absolutely unbearable. When I bring it to your attention, you grin and kiss me. It is your way to say thank you for noticing. But you really don't care much that you have been blessed with such a beautiful face and body. And I love that about you. You care about the things that really matter.

The lines at the corners of your eyes are so exquisite. Yes, you are aging... I have never seen anyone do it so wonderfully as you. You just keep getting better. Each line represents a road you've traveled or a love you've shared, maybe a temptation you have passed by. The most recent ones are for me. I am on your face. How completely glorious!

Did you know that you grin and crinkle your brow as you dream? And sometimes you moan... maybe when you are dreaming of me, or at least that's what feels right. Often you smile or chuckle in your sleep. Me again, perhaps.

I said to you last night, "What if we have to part?"

I want you to know what your response meant to me.

You said, "Then we will always have this moment, and we'd better give it all we have... as if it were our last."

And then you touched my face so gently, with such a look, as I have never seen in you. But I suddenly and silently understood that this is how you live every moment with me... as if it were our last. Now I know fully and steadfastly how deeply and honestly you love me.

Like you, I don't know what our futures will bring... our situation is awkward at best and I am amazed that we see each other at all, but we mesh in a way I have never meshed before. I'd follow you to the ends of the earth if you asked me. I've never said that before. My two ex-husbands will confirm this. Will I ever say it again... to you? Yes.

As I watch the exquisite magnitude of all that you are stretched out in front of me, I am aware of God. You are a masterpiece of flawed perfection, like an ageless marble statue or the magnificence of old raw Chinese silk. Even your goofy laughter is God laughing through you.

How will I ever thank you for digging through the grapevine to find me? Isn't it amazing to think that one twist of the plan could have changed it all and maybe we would not have crossed paths? I am happy you were determined to chase every butterfly with your net.

You are my prince. Grand, elegant, rugged, goofy, brilliant, defiant, forgetful, teasingly tempting, tender, stern, creative, abstract, spiritual, sensuous, the dreamer, the doer... the man who makes magic.

How will I tell you how beautiful you are? How will you believe me? I will show you. I will show you with every glance, every kiss and every word, every touch, until you see yourself through my eyes. If we must part... these moments, and all that have come before will be frozen in me, held suspended in time and space.

You said you have known me for lifetimes. I believe you. If it is true, and we do part, then we will meet again if we agree to it now.

So the question is not if I will be with you, my dear man, it is shall I be with you forever? Would I take that risk? Can you guess my answer?

What is our plan together in this lifetime? I am not sure of that, but I know that when I am with you I am grateful. Ahhh... dear sweet prince... you are so beautiful.

This man and I have not been able to spend much time together and may never be able to, but that certainly is not the point. The point is energy, what has happened when we have been together. When you see a relationship as an entity to give your best to, it can be occupied with the production of miracles. More than you at any time imagined possible.

I have discovered that writing to a lover deepens the alliance and makes it more real and rooted. You might say more on paper than you would verbally. Even people who have been together a long time often find that writing to each other opens closed or never before opened doors.

Also, leave little notes around that start with the words: What I love about you is... and finish the sentence in as many ways as you can think of for that day. It is okay if you repeat yourself on different days. Another good one is: I love you because... and finish it as distinctly as possible.

I love you because...

You touch me and my heart quakes.

You respect me, even when I am angry.

You are wonderful to me even when I am as mad as a rattlesnake!

You ran my perfect bath and then joined me.

You overcooked the lobster because you were distracted with me.

You are a treasure, *my* treasure.

Or

You help me to remember how lucky I am to have ever met you.

The idea here is to say what is true for you. Never make up something that is not true for you... it won't feel good. That is deceptive, not loving. Be as elaborate or as simple as you like, but do the thing. Listen. Write.

I have numerous love letters from my daughter and from men I have loved. Some wrote poetry. Every word ever written by any one of them is golden.

Love notes and letters ground you to a bigger Self. They get you to notice things often overlooked. This makes your life richer in a way that no other activity can. Even making love with your special lover can not compare to a love letter from your lover. Take my word on this one... I know of what I speak.

I look forward to writing many love letters to the man I eventually take the plunge for. He's got to be worth the big dive into the deep end. Will it be the man who's letter you just read? We will see. That may not be the plan. But if it is not, the man who comes along will definitely want to love my letters. He's got to be open hearted like that. How will I know what is in the plan? It will unfold before me in its own time and its own way. He will literally be unearthed from the hidden universe that surrounds us all.

A note about the giving of your love letters... one man did not enjoy receiving my oh-so-special letters, my Costner look alike. My first one was a lovely letter, what is called a *living letter,* that states what will always be true for you about that person beyond the seen. It is a farseeing spiritual gift that is not given lightly or without great thought. He read it and thanked me as if I'd given him a bit of my dinner. Wooooosh... right over the head and heart! Direct miss. That was that. It went into a drawer and stayed there, not to be treasured, but purely to be set aside and saved as something unique.

Ouch!

So, a word toward mindfulness... take the time to be certain that your lover appreciates what you are doing and is excited to participate. Love letters are to be adored and read over and over year after year. That's part of their beauty. Wrap passionately colored ribbons around them and keep the ones you receive until the day you leave this earth, perhaps a fiery red or royal blue with gold. Leave them to your children, but be sure that you and your lover don't hold back anything... each word will be precious. Your kids will know that you have loved and been loved. And they will learn to love deeper, too. They need that.

We are all that curious and fragile at a deep level rarely recognized. They will respect that you shared this of yourself.

By the way, as a side note, I suspect Kevin loves love letters. It's a hunch. Don't quote me on it. My ex-lover looks like him, but that's all. Otherwise, I suspect they are worlds apart, extreme in their differences. The look alike never got another love letter from me. Today I won't be with a man who has that sort of knee-jerk reaction I described, it means he has a hidden agenda that will come up and bite me like a rattler. Want to see my scars? Again, trust me on this one.

Men are wonderful creations… I adore them, but we ladies do need to take care of and honor ourselves. We must be good to ourselves and in no way abusive to others.

The truth is quite simple, really. You are worth the most sacred and most generous relationship imaginable. Writing a love letter will, at the least, let you know your boundaries with your lover if you don't know them now.

And let's face it, if you are not romantic about your partner, you aren't seriously in love with that person. I'd put money on that one.

If your child gives you a love letter, put it in a spot where you will see it over and over. I guarantee smiles. Lots of smiles, on their faces and yours.

Dear Mom,

Hiya!!! I'm in 5th period!! Oh joy and bliss! So, are you feeling any better? I hope you are!! Well, I'm having an ok day.

Well, I have to go now.

Love you muchly,
Katie

p.s. I love you!!!!!!!

Kate wrote these words years ago. I keep this note above my computer. It is special and beautiful, like she is.

When she found out about this book, she faxed me the following love letter. I cried for an hour.
Want to know what your children are thinking about you?
Teach them early to go to the page.
You will reap the rewards.

A Testament to the Woman I Love

Katie Wormald

Printed by permission... actually, by demand.

Throughout the past 18 years of my life, one woman has been there for every heartache, every tear, and every laugh... so many special moments have been shared between us. No matter how upset she might get with me, she always let me know that she still loved me just as much as before she got mad.

When I was 5 my parents got a divorce. My brother stayed mostly with my Dad and I stayed with my Mom. Things were hard for us; we always got through them. Every problem, every disappointment... she always made it work out. I have always admired her for this. She would put her life on hold for me... her child, although now I wish she hadn't.

I am Kathaleen Rachelle Wormald, Katie or Kate for short. I am the daughter of one of the most beautiful women in the world, Ms. Lee Travathan. She raised me to know more about life than I think she even knows. She is my best friend and mother.

When I was having a problem, I knew she would be there to help me get through it. For example, in 1998 I almost did not graduate high school due to a counselor who did not have enough faith in me. My mom gave me the confidence to say, "Screw that! I am going to graduate from this school!" And a week later I did, along with many others. I am so happy to say that she pushed me to do it, to stand up for myself. Because of her love and support I am now in my second year of college.

I am very proud of her and I know she will do very well in whatever project she takes on. I deeply admire her and wish her only the best of luck. Which I know she will have.

Mommy… I love you and thank you for everything you have done for me in the past 18, now almost 19, years. Now it is your time to follow your dreams as you have helped me to do. I am me because of you. Thank you, Mom. I would not want any other mother. You are my inspiration.

Your one and only,
~Katie~

P.S. You go get 'em, Tiger!

It is true… you never know what your kids are thinking until they tell you.
I will treasure this gift for eternity.

Exercise: Go to the page. Listen for a love letter that wants to be written. Don't think; listen.

If you do not have or want a lover, let a love letter to yourself come through. You deserve scads of these!

Blatant Disregard

He [man] is a social microcosm, reflection on the smallest scale the quantities of society at large, or, conversely, as the smallest social unit, cumulatively producing the collective dissociation. The latter possibly is the more likely one, as the only direct and concrete carrier of life is the individual personality, while society and the State are conventional ideas and can claim reality only is so far as they are represented by a certain number of individuals.

Carl Jung

Rebel writers express a blatant disregard for the standard rules of writing... and often for the same of life in general. Thank goodness, literally.

The basic rules for effective writing are simple, and excessively limiting. Think, plan, and organize before your first draft. After; revise, revise, revise. Keep your titles accurate and specific, clear and concise. No wonder more people don't write! What a scary proposition! Effective writing is some of the most boring and arduous writing I've ever read. It lulls me to sleep. And it hangs creativity.

Rebel writing is the opposite. Since it is not rooted in placing something *on* the page, but is intended to deliver something *out of* the page through listening, it is a further highway entirely.

By violating the rules you will induce free writing, raw writing, way-down-at-the-bottom-of-the-river writing. You will dive deep and swim unrestrained.

Rebel writing allows you to dance with the page and permit it to show you which move to give rise to next. It knows. It will tell you the steps of the dance. It may make up a new dance or enrich on an old one. It will allow you to meander and stroll about effortlessly.

Meandering is essential to rebel writing. You go to the page and let yourself roam around; writing whatever comes up for your viewing pleasure. You need not know what that will be, but you must disregard the common rules of writing to arrive there. If you follow the rules of effective writing, you are dead at first stop.

Think. Rebel writers don't think; they listen. They don't tell the story, the story tells itself. Rebels are instruments. Receivers of thought. Universal thought.

Plan. Oh, please! To plan the writing is to build a diversion dam between you and the story that is trying to tell itself. Enter writer's block. Teenagers who don't plan anything write some of the best writing I read. They simply free associate. It is pure genius. When I read writing that is "well planned", it is often stuffy, dull, and severely rigid. No surprises, no amusement. No emotions other than boredom. Clearly not my cup of tea.

Organize. Frustration is stepping in already. Again, stuffy. Lifeless. Too neat and orderly.

Revise, revise, and revise. May I jump off the Empire State building yet? Chopping up your piece into bits will leave you with little. Usually your first instincts are either true or a step to a bigger picture, not a smaller one. You merely need to make sure that your thoughts are easy to follow as you edit. If you make sense when you talk, you will make sense on the page.

Effective writing does not allow for meandering, dancing, synchronicities, miracles, magic, surprises, raw emotions, sentence fragments, double exclamation marks, odd and quirky cosmic occurrences; in short - forget the universal breadcrumb trail. Clearly, it leaves no room to confer with dishes, or God, or hang with angels. It bounds genius… your genius. Yes, you are an unclaimed genius. Didn't anyone tell you that? It's true. There will be more on that in the next book, Rebel Writer Two.

Okay, so I may get some nasty letters over this chapter from schoolteachers and university professors that teach effective writing, but that's to be expected. I am breaking the mold with this book and some risks come with the choice I've made. My contact info is in the back of the book if you would like to comment.

This book is writing itself. A filmmaker friend called this morning to say that she received my sample chapters and couldn't put them down. She wanted more, now! I fired off a few faxed pages as we talked.

"Whoa, girl! What have you done? It dances! It dances and it moves me. I grin as I read about your guys. I cry about your past. I am astonished by your thoughts! I laugh at your humor! Why can't I write like this?" she pouted.

"You can. Don't just read the pages, Silly Goose, do what they say. Listen. Write," I bluntly retorted.

"But it's too simple, too easy. When I buy a screenplay and pay the big bucks, the writer should earn it. Right? I thought writing involved the sweat of the brow and all that. Like, you have to be really smart and talented. You know, have a gift."

"Yes. You have to be able to listen. Listening *is* the gift." She sighed in confusion. "Can you hear me right now?" I asked.

"Of course."

"Now, close your eyes and tell me… can you hear me if I am quiet for a moment?" I asked the question and then paused.

"Yes, you're still there, clear as a bell!"

"Then you can hear the page."

She thought a moment. "You know the critics will eat you alive on this one, don't you? Just the way they eat Costner for dinner when he makes a knock out movie that means something important."

I did not respond. I am not so sure they will notice.

"Oh! Oh! Did you know that *Heaven* and *Kevin* rhyme?" she chuckled. Now, that's a fan!

"Oh, like you think that matters," I answered in a deadpan voice. "You had to do that didn't you… you just could not let me get through one day… ugh!"

She interrupted me. "You're cute. Hey, the *thing* is beyond chance. Deal with it."

She laughed. I growled gently.

"Yeah, right. Talk to you later. Now, leave me alone. I've got a book to write… to hear."

I shook off the *thing* as best I could and went on with my day.

But I am compelled to entertain the truth that her silliness was sweet and cute, even endearing. She was meandering in her speech like rebel writers do on the page, adding a little ditty for the sake of interest. She just spit it out, the thought, the same way that the page spits out a new thought in the middle of current abstraction.

I thought to myself, she actually has time to think about that stuff? Darn it, I thought out loud… she got me! I won't be able to get that silly rhyme out of my head all day now. I'll have to write about it till it's all written *out*! Hmm… interesting.

My friend, within the balance of her cute sort of nature, is right. This book may appall the critics of modern literature. This book means something, something important that matters. It means that you have been misinformed, at the least, lesser informed, about the practice of writing and its methodology. But that's no one's fault… we are an evolving species. The rules of effective writing were a good start for those who felt the need to be strictly organized; it was a place to leap from, but they are not good for the whole of the creative writing community. They are not a good place for rebels to stay.

I wonder how many years have passed that you believed you are not a writer. For most, it is far too many. There is a process of recovery and rediscovery to relax into now. Your quiet trauma can be over.

Like I said, rebels write for the whole, whether they intend to or not. They break the rules to present something new and important… and yes, they do rock the boat, too. Even if it is only their own boat. Why? They must.

Things that can't be seen are still happening. We are far too frequently drowning in our own reserved unconscious suppression.

What if most of what you were taught about writing is not true? Would you write?

I am giving you permission to write the backbone *out* of your page and *out* of your life. I am unlocking the chains of your self-imposed prison. You are at liberty to unlock your safety belts and move freely about the page. Write. Be sloppy. Be controversial if you need. Break the rules. It will all work in the final spin cycle.

If you don't have permission to make a mess on the page, you may not go there at all. This is much like finger painting time in kindergarten. Let Go. Go ahead. Step forward. Make a mess. Get dirty. It's okay. The more messes you make in the beginning the less you will make later.

You see, the thing is to just get to the page and listen. It does not have to be toilsome drudgery, the sweat of the brow and all that. Go daily and simply see what the page would like to say. Take at least thirty minutes, more if you have it. It is not important to make a big deal out of it. Write longhand or use the computer. Write anywhere.

Rebel writers are typically not "dutiful" writers who sit in a room designed just for writing with all their little pencils neatly sharpened, sitting in the perfect chair with the perfect reference books staring them blankly them in the eyes. They don't need to be dutiful and strictly disciplined or obsessive and rigid. What they require is the freedom to roam the page and discover its contents.

Rebel writing is the smooth transition of one moment moving fluidly into another, a meander through a field of wildflowers, or a Sunday drive with a hitchhiking idea that just happens to catch your eye and your fancy. It is a journey into an extraordinary universe of mystical creation, not a task for your already ego-burdened and weary ordinary self. Put ordinary aside for wonderful and see what transpires.

Make it easy. It is already. Listen... simply listen. Write what you hear.

As a rule, when a story is finished, and certainly always by the time it is published, I have no recollection of the various phases of its development.

Dorothy Canfield

Personal Notes:

Take Loving Care of Your Writer

Pavlov's advice on how to succeed – "Passion and gradualness." Even in those areas where we have already developed a high degree of skill, it sometimes helps to drop back, lower our sights a bit, and practice with a feeling of ease.

This is especially true when one reaches a sticking point in progress, where effort for additional progress is unavailing.

Continually straining to beyond the sticking point is likely to develop undesirable "feeling habits" of strain, difficulty, effort.

Maxwell Maltz

It is Saturday morning, July 10, 1999, two minutes after ten. Instantly upon waking today this book told me that it is a stone's throw to wrapping and it wants to start the process of slow descent. It will gradually take me out of marathon mode now… easing me into the global distribution landing position like a 747 floating onto the LAX runway with only a splendid hum in the background and the occasional tinny click of a seatbelt belatedly being fastened by a rebel. It is a seductive image embedded into a raw and perfectly unpolished feeling.

My mind flooded with everything that it has stirred in my soul since the book began to write itself, and what I will be left to face once it is complete. A plethora of emotions, comfortable and uncomfortable, have gently migrated upward then jetted forward in consciousness equitably through the precise act of bold commitment. This always happens when I scrawl a script or book. Post delivery blues begin just toward the end and hit vigorously at the very last word typed.

I hear my mind wondering, oh God, what have I done? For a moment I can barely believe that I produced what I hold in my hands. It can knock me right off my feet.

It is the way the piece tells me that my life will change... again. And I will be a different woman than the single-minded woman who became pregnant with the project and gave it life on the page. I will be made anew and I will shed the old. I will have increased responsibilities and opportunities. And though, at times, it will appear that my butt is getting whipped out there in the world, I am actually being made stronger and more useful to the world as a whole.

"It is time to part the Red Sea again, Babe," a loving actor friend stated earlier over the phone.

And I can do it. He *knows* I can. I've had plenty of practice. When the book is finished, I will need a long and quiet day to just be with it and nurse it like a newborn, just the two of us. It will spend nearly all of the day in my arms and hands, being caressed and cooed over. I will thank it for docking in this space called my life and stand in open gratitude to my creator for bringing it. I'll be on my knees quite often. Then it will be time to ask a few close industry friends and angels to do a blessing with me; the way we do for their movies, books, or television shows. We ask that the message be what God intended.

Then I part the Red Sea... I divide the past and the present that I can be more centered in the now.

The sea is the ocean of my emotions. It has been called the *Red Sea* as a commentary to my long flaming red hair that actually has five colors ranging from black to red to blonde, and my now and then flaming Irish temper that is ever so easily tamed with a few hugs and kisses. And because when I need to be recklessly direct, I can make people's hearts tremble and their legs shake. "Give the woman anything she wants!" they shudder in panic. That's when I know it's time to re-evaluate myself. It is also in reference to my deeply acute consciousness that senses balance like a foxhunter and needs that balance in my everyday life.

When the sea must be parted and the old and worn out parts sent to the bottom, that's when the actual work of the book begins. The publisher may have put the book to bed, but I now have pieces of my life puzzle to section together that have come foaming up from the torrent of activity that the book was.

This narrows down to taking care of myself, emotionally, physically, mentally and spiritually. It is a time to accept the things I have not wanted to look at or integrate into my life. To face the forbidden fears cowering in the dark cobwebby corners of my shadowed inner spaces.

This is the time of heartfelt evolution on the trail of the true human being. This is where life gets larger, fuller, and more *mine.* Here, today on the page, ownership of the Extraordinary Self will take precedence over all other things as the labor towards delivery begins. And yes, there it is… what I did not know before I began writing today. *I am in labor.* It has started here and now.

The baby is coming into the world soon. Intensely soon. Just a few chapters to push through and I will behold a whole child, fingers and toes. I will cognize what it casts before me.

Here, I become romantic about the book and my secret life with it while missing the men that I have not seen since I became pregnant with the book 18 days ago. What I'd give right now for a prolonged involved kiss, dripping with affection and strong warm hairy arms around me all afternoon. In me is a kissaholic of the truest sort and today I am intensely alert to the cravings that haunt my lips and remind me of kisses past, as well as the compulsion to be kissed and stroked just now. I admit to being a lush about such things. Such a craving and longing rests here now in me that I will not act upon and I already sense the day as long and slow, teasing me into a temptation that I clearly must resist. No… it would do no good to give into to it today.

"Who the hell is this woman, this Lee Travathan. Lee… Lee… what kind of a name is that for a lanky sexy woman with a conspicuous striking beauty and loads of charisma?" the page interrupts to dispose my mind elsewhere. The page is biased like a doting parent.

"It's my middle name," I tell the page. I don't use my first name as it conjures up images of the Deep South and distracts everyone from my sincere purpose. In the end, I have to silently admit to myself that deep down I am really Scarlet and her opposite ego all mixed into one: thunder and fire, passion and demanding ambition, gentleness and sweetness.

I wouldn't hurt a fly but I'll write the pants off any man alive! And I will make movies that storm the soul with passion and courage instead of those no-brain bullflicks where you just blast people apart or rip off their clothes! The personality of thunder and soft rain… it's a crisis of a combination to get stuck with. Drives men wild, but then they get so excited that they really don't see *me*… the me under all that.

It's like having a hot role in a blockbuster movie and then attempting to convince the still hypnotized audience that you really are another person off the screen. By that time, they are so enamoured that they are blinded by lust.

I could have lived Gone With The Wind… the Deep South. I think I had a few lifetimes there. I have family there now who wouldn't leave it for all the gold still hidden in the hills of California. It's excellent for them, but it could never be enough refuge for me. I'd always yearn for Hollywood. What a paradox. A southern name and an itch for fame. Funny, I never admitted to myself before now that I still harbor a fancy for fame. I'm not sure I consciously knew it all that clearly until just this very moment.

"Yeah, you're a puzzle, alright. And now that you have unearthed a few lost pieces while writing this book, what will you do with them?" the page is asking in the manner of a muse.

I know the answer. I must find out where those pieces fit. I question where I will place the elusive man in my life that I sense and feel and talk to on the page. Since I have not discovered him in the physical, where *will* I rest that piece? And what will be encircling it? How do I relate and fit in a piece that I can't see with my naked eye? And what of my first name? Will I exact it only for my intimate relationships or drop it all together? I can't let go quite yet… the unseen man on the way loves that name. I suspect he has a slight touch of redneck in his system. It is not much, he was not born into it, so it is only enough to make him a little goofy and give him an occasional unconscious draw.

And what of my present intimate relationships? Suddenly, today, I feel they are spent, that what we have encountered, without speaking of it, are different roads to travel. And our ways will soon be parted. What then? What does an extremely selective kissaholic do without a lover? Nothing. And what is that like? What is nothing like? I kind of remember. When I lived in Charlottesville, Virginia, I was without a lover for two years.

Oh, why did I remember that? I suddenly feel sick. It was dreadful. I wasn't willing to sleep with just anyone so I slept alone. No one there stirred my heart. It was a long and drawn-out two years of intense kiss deprivation. Pure hell.

And there is that room downstairs boasting and bulging of exercise equipment that I don't use… I almost never walk in there, even when it calls to me. The hill calls me to come stroll more often and type less. Will I listen now that the book is descending onto the runway?

I look at my body imaged into the large mirrors of my bedroom and give it my approval. I don't look 44. I look between 28 and 30, and I wish to maintain this gift for as long as I can. Yes, I'd better make friends with this body more intimately than I have. The time is now. It requires my love and attention; the exercise equipment is terribly lonely. It is a sad situation. I never want to be sad over my body. I will love it much better than I have as soon as the birth is over. I will bring my body and the equipment together. Yes. It's a deal. I am a matchmaker.

And there is always the *Thing* to deal with. More prayer… more prayer. Answers. I need answers. I turn it all over to God… every little tid-bit every single day.

I need to be better about eating too, I forget to do it. I need to have someone follow me around when I'm working and feed me the right foods like Irene does sometimes. Yes, I like that idea. It's that or liquid food all day long.

"And what of your spirit?" the page gently moans like a strong wind through a hollow red canyon in the Southwest. It has a tap on my energy today so it is being especially seductive in the absence of a lover, overly accommodating.

I will have given birth to a book that will always bare my name and be a part of my lineage. It is a spiritual entity of sorts. I am a spiritual being first, a mind second, and a body third. In essence, the book and I have much in common.

The page is asking me to voice what is missing in my life... to face it and coax it from the dark corners of forbidden thought. For this is the real spiritual issue... what *is* missing? What have I not given myself?

Love. Enough love. I did not expect this response from my own mind.

I am not in love with the men I see, not actually. And I have not pretended to be in love with any one of them. That's the truth I refused to witness. Many things... I love about them. I cherish them. I adore them. I treasure them. I enjoy each moment. They are important to me. But would I spend my life with any one of them were they to ask me today? No. And therein lies the truest test of love.

They have not failed. I have not failed. Some things are simply not in the plan.

He is out there somewhere, and until he is my friend he will never be my lover. I may encounter many male friends before I am led to the right guy. I never wanted to believe that there was a *right* guy. I was wrong. There is a right guy, at least for me; I now understand the depth of this simple truth.

So I have come to the page today to discover a concealed or secret truth... I want to love more deeply than I ever have before and be loved more deeply than I have let myself be. I feel this truth in my heart as if a branding iron were searing it slow and hard into the fleshy membrane. And I don't like its face. It scares me. It is raw and open truth that involves risks I have not taken before. But it would be weak of me not to face it. Looking into its laser like eyes takes me past "uncomfortable" and I feel a certain sort of agony coming on quickly, as well as a sense of relief. Ah, so maybe I'll get it right this lifetime!

I do not miss or long for a missing part, as if some man could come along and fill an empty place (I am not an empty space), but I have unconsciously missed giving the fullness and richness of my love. I am good with men, meaning I do relationship unusually well. I exceed at loving. I don't care to waste that talent on a bunch of creative excuses.

That's what I miss... another clue is uncovered. I miss the breath on the back of my neck as I drift off to sleep and the awareness of a deserving man resting alongside me. I miss sharing my day with a man that matters to me.

As much as I have loved, I have not loved enough. I have not given all that God has given me to share. At some point I let the strong woman in me lead; the "gutsy spitfire", as a good friend calls it, believes that she does better without a commitment to a man. Wrong again. I do okay, but I don't do all that extremely *well.* The hidden truth, the real truth, is that it is a great excuse to bet that I won't get hurt. I had no idea that I had hidden this ache deep inside so well, even from myself. Now as it surfaces, it is brand new and delicate.

The truth looms heavy over my eyes. Here it is in black and white. In all honesty, I think life without a commitment to a lover sucks rotten eggs. It is not that it is lonely; I don't feel lonely, but it is just a lesser life than I can have.

I will take care of myself and my passionate writer better than I have been on all these levels as the book begins to land onto the runway for disembarking and I head toward the delivery station. We deserve the attention. And I will let go of the fear-based concept that I don't need a man to make me happy. It is a defense mechanism and it is only partially true.

What I have kept hidden is the knowledge that I sincerely enjoy men and I'd love a close love that I could care about as much as I care about myself. I am excited about spending the rest of my life with me. I know what a blessing and treasure that is. I'd like to feel that way about a wonderful man, too.

Rebel writing will indeed shift where you are in unconscious moments. I have been surprised by the words of change today. This is not what I thought I would write, but it is what needed to be written. And faced.

Raw rebel writing like this shows you where your life is out of balance and attempts to correct it, you are that valuable to your creator who speaks through the page. And in the grand scheme of things that creator never underestimates your value and purpose, only people do that.

Take care of your writer. He or she deserves your kind love and attention. Your writer is a precious servant who desires to serve you. Take care of it and you and it will serve you for life.

Exercise: Go to the page. Ask it how you can take better care of yourself. Let it meander, it needs to have that leeway. Be willing to face what you would not acknowledge before the exercise.

Live your beliefs and you can turn the World around.
Henry Thoreau

The Voices of Angels

For He shall give His angels charge over thee, to keep thee in all thy ways. They shall bear thee up in their hands, lest thou dash thy foot against a stone.

Psalms 91: 11, 12

The above verse is a promise; not a grouping of words crafted to flow well or sound pleasing to the ear when read aloud. It is a statement of commitment, like a marriage vow. It is the creator saying, “I take thee.” The angels are the creator’s wedding gift to you. If you choose to accept the angels’ mission in your life, you will be the receiver of constant miracles. This I know to be factual based on experience.

When you go to the page and ask for divine guidance it will come. I use this guidance for my own needs, the needs of friends and those I love. I ask to talk to angels, Jesus, or God often, and receive answers that astound me while giving me peace and comfort. There is no unique way to do this. Simply ask, listen and write. Know that they are there waiting in the page. Anyone can do this. It takes no special talent.

One of my desires for rebel writing is that it reconnects us to our source at its deepest applications. We’ve had the ability to do this, just like the writers of the Bible and for as long, lifetimes. But our ego(s) and its tool, logic, make us slow to comprehend the perfection of the universe. Consciousness has not raised to a level that allows our gifts to be openly acceptable. How do we raise consciousness? We begin to apply what we know. We grow and expand our understanding.

Why do most people believe that they can’t talk to angels, or Jesus, or God, and get answers? That only certain people can do that? Conditioning. You can transform this conditioning in your life and that will change the life itself into something greater.

I take God's promises very seriously. I learned long ago that of myself I can do nothing. With God, I can do anything. For me, this is not a Bible issue, it is a life tool. I pray for something to be handled and it is handled, it is as simple as that. I realize that we are simply receiving stations for thought while being a species with power and dominion over all things.

I say these things to you that you will know you can talk to those mentioned here no matter what your situation or circumstance. Your race or religion does not matter. There is actually nothing to stand in your way but you. If you think it odd that people do these things, you are already blocking your own view. The best way to clear that block is to sit down and practice listening to the voices of angels. Write what you hear.

It is our birthright to hear the love and support of the universe. Don't let that be taken away from you and don't take it from yourself. It is too precious to set aside out of ignorance.

Give yourself the gifts that you came here to receive. They are your birthrights.

Partswork for Rebel Writers

If you have found fault with any part of yourself, you have misunderstood your teachers. All that you experience is a part of you attempting to gain your attention... neither good nor bad.

You all possess the same parts; all acting out their prescribed roles in the play called life. What you would call tragedy we would call a wake up reminder. What you call drama we call passion. What you call evil we call your unfaced fears. Face your fears and they will no longer own you, you will own them. You will own yourself. Nothing God made is evil... it is simply misunderstood energy that will become just about anything you wish it to be. You are in control, as you possess the mind of God in your mind.

Know the lost, lonely, hidden and misguided parts of self and you will be actualized. Under the lays of logic you know them well. Now, uncover and discover that which serves you... your parts system... the very servants of God to help you shape your lives.

Taken from The Angel Pages

When I began to comprehend that there is nothing in me that is bad, I was sure all was well in the world, no matter what my eyes saw. And I was correct.

Rebel writers have a wonderful tool at their access. They can talk to all their parts and learn what each part is doing then reroute it if they choose to do so.

When something is happening in your life that is not to your liking you're either dealing with a timing issue or a parts issue.

A timing issue arises when we are attempting to make something happen in our mental time frame. We forget that the universe has our blueprint and it knows exactly what we set up in our perfect plan, the plan that is also God's plan for us. The universe will follow that blueprint; not allowing our petty wants and needs to mess up the entire scheme of things we arranged during our undiluted genius period prior to birth. We are that loved.

When a part gets out of order in the system and you can't find peace, it is a part that is attempting to get your attention. It is time to talk to the part and generate a new understanding for it, like a parent does with a small child.

The parts are not good or bad, they just exist as our servants in the life plan. They execute plays, tap into your intuition if you're close to the edge of the cliff, and bring elements of your dreams to your attention. In short, they are academy award caliber actors on the stage that is your mind and your life. They act out any part that they deem important for your growth.

Partswork is gone into in much more detail in my workshops than it is here, but I will give you a taste that can start you on track to do it yourself. If I went into it much deeper, it would be another book. It is quite involved. Since we have brought an application of it to light with Gary and his dishes earlier, we will go on to a few other less dominating examples taken from typical everyday situations that are self-explanatory.

Partswork can be directive or non-directive. The important questions that are used over and over in each partswork session are highlighted in bold print.

Part of me that is attempting to communicate by making me tired right now, **what do you want me to hear?** (Directive: specifying a particular part. When you use this method, insert any element in question.)

Part: Well, there you are. Man, you can really be slow, you know that? I've been making you tired for about an hour now so you will get my message. You shouldn't be going out with that guy tonight.

Lee: Why not? I like him. He's sweet... I think. Hum... suddenly, I'm not so sure.

Part: He's a big Hollywood ado that you'll be wiser to have nothing to do with. He is literally much to do about nothing in context to your life. You have no plan with him beyond today.

Lee: Cute. Okay, give it up. What's the big deal? It's just a date.

Part: Not for him. He's got plans of his own. He has not discussed them with you.

Lee: Like?

Part: Going to his place, alone. And then you'll never see the guy again. It is his way… slay 'em and leave 'em. That way you'll never forget him. He likes to leave a little sting, like a rubber band on the wrist someone trying to stop smoking.

Lee: No, I wouldn't do that. Go to his place? On a first date? I don't know him that well. He's a friend of a friend.

Part: Yeah, well, he does not care about that. He's gonna try to trick you. But don't take my word for it…

Lee: Well, he is acting a little odd today. Not being specific about tonight. Maybe you're on to something here. But really, I can just tell him that I don't want to do that.

Part: That's not really the biggest issue. You see, you are only going out of a general curiosity, which you don't feel too great about. You don't really care anything about this guy. In fact, your gut tells you to let it go. This guy is not your cup of tea. You love to see him on the big screen and you respect his talent… why not just leave it there?

Deep down you know you will just be disappointed. The guy is not very kind. He isn't respectful and he won't be good to you. Can I put it more bluntly? The guy has some real control parts out of order in his system. You're gonna get very disappointed if you go tonight. In fact, you'll be back here in less than an hour.

Lee: Are you sure that you aren't being just a little over protective? I am a big girl. I can handle myself.

Part: I am protecting you. It's my job. Do you really want to go out with this guy?

Lee: I am curious.

Part: I will ask again. Do you really want to go out with this guy? Trust your gut.

Lee: Ah! It said "No!" Big No! I'm going to call him and press him on the plans for tonight. (I left the page and made a call to his cell phone.) Well, you had it right. He was cooking dinner at his house and preparing his bedroom for me to stay there tonight.

Part: Sure wish I had put some money on this one. Wasn't too happy you aren't coming is he?

Lee: Not happy at all. In fact, he was quite rude about it. Yeah, I think I will just leave him on the big screen where he belongs. This would have gotten pretty gnarly tonight. He was awkwardly pushy over the phone; it just did not feel good to me.

Part: Look, if it was another guy and he was a solid man, had his head together, and was thinking of you in a heart-felt way, I might have steered you in another direction. Don't give up, kiddo. There are good guys in Hollywood. Trust that. You'll run across the right one or he will run across you. Just keep checking in. I'm always hanging out, open to talk. So you won't be tired now. I was just trying to protect you, keep you from going. I figured if you got too tired…

Lee: Right. Hey, **Thanks for the help**. I needed it. And I'm not tired any longer. I had this guy pegged all wrong. Guess I bought some of the hype, huh? (The part grins. I can sense this in my mind.) Don't give me a hard time, he was rather seductive. And he looks so good on the screen. Hey, thanks for the encouragement. **Is there anything else you need to say?**

Part: Yes. You're going to be all right with this relationship stuff. You know that, don't you?

Lee: Most of the time. I have my rough days. I long to give the love I have. I don't want to just dump it on someone; I want to meet the right friend first. That really matters to me.

Part: And if it moves quickly? From friendship to…

Lee: I pray that I am courageous enough and wise enough to go for it.

Part: Yeah, your okay.

Lee: **Thanks again**.

As you can see, I was saved from a rough night. The protective part induced the tiredness to communicate and when it said what was needed, the fatigue lifted. I ended up seeing a friend that night who told me the man in question had a bad habit of seducing women over dinner at his place, having them stay over and then never returning their calls. That would, indeed, sting.

This next example is from several years ago when I was involved with the movie star look alike I have mentioned. This time a part was not seemingly acting on my behalf and needed guidance.

Part that is keeping me in this relationship, what are you attempting to communicate? What do you want me to know? (You can be a little loose on this opening question as long as you are asking for the correct information.)

Part: But I will be all alone if he leaves. I don't want to be alone. (This part had a soft child-like voice. That meant it was an old and unresolved part. It had not matured with the rest of the system. A fear had not been handled.)

Lee: **How old are you**?

Part: Six.

Lee: **Are you alone**?

Part: All alone. Nobody wants me. But Dan, (not his real name… this name just popped up right now.) he wants me. He even loves me. He calls me *baby*. He sees me in you.

Lee: Oh, yes, he's very drawn to you in me. But I need you to understand something important. **Are you listening**?

Part: That's all I do is listen. Nobody ever talks to *me*. Nobody even knows I am here.

Lee: Well, I am talking to you right now and I need you to really hear me. Did you know that this relationship with Dan is hurting me?

Part: I hear you cry sometimes.

Lee: Yes. Quite often, I am very, very, sad. He does hurtful things because he is very angry with women. And so he gets angry with me even when I am doing nothing to upset him. When I want to let it go, I sense you creating a feeling of neediness in me that keeps me there. I don't like that. I need to let this man go and I need your faithful assistance in achieving this goal. I can't fill the empty spaces in him or heal his contempt for other women. Do you see that?

Part: Uh huh… but I don't want to be alone. I don't want to feel unloved and unwanted. It hurts.

Lee: Well, now that you have exposed yourself, I will love you. I want you. You are not alone. You are a part of me. **Do you know how old I am**?

Part: Six?

Lee: No, I am 39.

Part: (The part is completely stunned.) That's old!

Lee: Not so old, but old enough to take better care of you than those people that raised me. I won't hurt you. **Is that all right with you**?

Part: I like that.

Lee: **Then you will help me to** let this relationship go?

Part: Okay.

Lee: **Thank you for your help. Is there anything else you need to say**?

Part: No.

Lee: **How old are you now**?

Part: 15. I want to rest now.

Lee: Okay. **Thanks again**.

As you can see, the part was young and afraid, stuck in a time when nobody wanted me. It did not understand that things had changed. And as its fear was eased it began to age.

This part never comes up anymore and I have not dialogued with it for quite a while. I can only suspect that it has integrated itself within the system at my current age. By doing this dialogue

I was able to let go of the dysfunctional relationship that was hurting me. It still was not easy, but it had seemed impossible prior to the dialogue. I no longer involve myself in "hit the wall" relationships with angry and contempt-filled men. I know I don't have to anymore. I got the lesson.

Relationships are one of our most difficult issues to handle as they expose more of us than typical friendships would. Here you can see how various elements can be managed on the page to offer guidance from your deep self.

The parts communicate off the page, too. When my daughter was born I had a tedious feeling about her health soon after delivery. The doctors begrudgingly checked her out again and again at my request and confirmed that she was absolutely fine, but Mom was being overly cautious. We took her home even though my gut was telling me she was not well.

On the second night I sat by her bassinet reading near the fireplace, feeling the need to stay at her side. It was late, nearly time for her last feeding. I was checking my watch when suddenly I heard a voice inside my head screaming, "Pick up the baby now!" It was urgent and concise. It was not a request; it was a demand. I grabbed Kate immediately to find that she was not breathing. Her body was limp, blue, and cold.

I screamed for help from her father and began attempts to get her breathing. We got to the hospital, just two miles away, and we were able to save her. It was fourteen long months before she was out of the woods and three years before she was home free. If it were not for the screaming voice in my head, a protective part or angel, Kate would have died on that second night at home.

Why are we so afraid to listen to our internal guidance system? Maybe it is a lack of education that keeps us in the dark and away from our highest good. We are so simple, and yet, miraculously complex. But clearly, we are magical beings set about onto a mystical sea full of wonder.

This book is here to help you try new things. Pick something from this chapter to apply to your own life. That's your assignment.

If you have a miracle or and angel story to share, let me know by faxing it to me. Info is in the back of this book. Thank You!

Personal Notes:

Clearing Pages

Life's fulfillment finds constant contradictions in its path; but those are necessary for the sake of its advance.

The stream is saved from the sluggishness of its current by the perpetual opposition of the soil through which it must cut its way. It is the soil which form its banks.

The Spirit of fight belongs to the genius of life.

Rabindranath Tagore

I miss my kids today something awful. My arms ache to touch them, my eyes yearn for the sight of their faces. My ears need to hear their unmistakable and uniquely individual voices. My arms also throb to hold my little eight-month-old granddaughter, Shy-shy, who will grow up to look like a mirrored counterpart of me, build and all. I'll show her how to listen to the page and rebel write early.

It is strenuous to groove into this longing and just let it be. I can't in effect; it's immoderately overpowering, so I take it to the page. I talk to the emotion in my clearing pages, the ones I whirl out of bed and scrawl out each day.

Clearing pages are my simple saviors when stress or any other uninvited guest hits my system. Or just when I want to clear the day for larger things. I go to the page and write about anything and everything that is on my mind, freely associating with any thought that arises. It does not matter what comes up or where it leads… clearing pages are the toxic waste dumpsites for the mind. The internal perfectionist is not acknowledged entry.

After writing about how I miss my kids this morning in these pages, I feel much improved, lighter. I still miss them, but it is more bearable. I know they miss me, too, and I will see them soon. Tonight I will call them both and promise that I will write to them more often. I need to do it for them and for me. Hollywood seems to be light years from San Diego today.

There is so much spinning around in this world that we don't say. I rebel against this with extreme and forceful intensity… I even have a soapbox, a real one, to stand on when I literally go into a full throttle mode.

I despise it that we leave so much life unsaid and that we are not brave enough to say what we mean and mean what we say. We can act like deplorable wimps, as I've done at times with the *Thing* and other issues in my life that make me shiver inside. It is not becoming of us and does not do justice to who and what we are under our masks, walls, and parade of lies that we maintain to keep ourselves sheltered from authentic intimacy.

I was recently with a prized friend who was on his way into surgery. At the last moment, when I leaned down to kiss him, he forcefully stuffed a soggy crumpled group of over-folded pages into my palm. With a kiss and a grin he said, "Just in case I don't come out of here alive… it's all the stuff I never told you that I should have told you." He passed out and was wheeled away.

I waited about an hour to read the pages; I had to let them dry. His words touched into a part of me that is the genius, the fighter, the lover, the friend, the sister, the mother, the filmmaker and artist, the rebel, the inspiration, the inspired, and the giver and taker of love. His words took shape in me as trembling and weeping I could not control.

Ire also rattled around in my chest as I wondered why we are so excessively dense when it comes to something as simple as speaking our personal truth to another. Millions of people pass away never letting their mouths sputter out the priceless words that could have rewritten a life.

Why don't we just say the words that will help heal us and make passionate enchantment of our lives? I believe it is because we can be chicken, timid about the reaction from another, and often apprehensive to meet the words ourselves. What we can't hear ourselves declare we can't utter to another.

So, today in my pages I let the longing splash out over the edges and drench me. I wrote about the miracles these human beings are to me, that I cherish every tiny element of their existence… how they move me in an unspeakable place. I am in love with my kids. They are the best things that I have ever done.

Once this was out of the page I was free to go into scheduling difficulties, make a mental note about what I need to grab from the store, and remember that I need to call a filmmaker to tell him in candid and undiluted words that I don't want to date him and why. I need to call a particular celebrity again either tomorrow or Tuesday about a book idea we discussed. And I must find out if the book I am doing on the hidden spiritual life of Hollywood can begin interviews in two weeks. I have to fit it between production of my upcoming movie as well as promo and workshops for this book.

All of this became *clear* on the clearing pages without procrastination. I like to do them first thing each day since they clear the space for other work that I will do with the page. They sweep the cobwebs out of my brain.

When all was said and done, I received an unexpected call from the friend who gave me the soggy pages. He caught me in a much-deserved bubble bath with candles all aglow.

"So what's shakin' today, pretty marathon woman?"

"I'm coming out of marathon mode and wrapping the book today and tomorrow afternoon. Would you believe I'm in a bubble bath right now?" He heard the relaxation in my voice and it made him happy. He chuckled.

"I knew I was in the wrong place today… knew it as soon as I woke up, yes indeed, I did," he teased. I laughed at his flirty silliness. "Alright, okay… I'll be a good boy… but ohhhhh, what a thought! Listen, about that note… may I write others like that, I mean, if I have a hard time saying the words?"

"Of course, you may," I assured him. He has a shy scuff-your-shoes-in-the-dirt side that I adore.

"I get so busy, you know, and I need to always be aware that I treasure you. I've dreamed of someone; maybe it was every time you… that I coveted the knowing of. I am so confounded and excited that you talk to me at all. How did I luck into this? Nobody I've known sees the world the way you do. It thrills me. You're a prize, the best friend I've ever had." He was quiet for a moment and I did not speak. "Wow! I said it! I have been wanting to say that for so long, and just that way."

I started crying he touched me so. I was talking to a 12-year-old boy in a fully adult body, a vastly accomplished man. It is one of the sweetest things in the world to have taken to heart that tingle in his voice. And to receive such an angelic compliment. I felt rhapsodic that I taught him to do clearing pages to help reduce stress. So many new doors have opened for us.

The clearing pages, when used as a dumpsite, open windows to the whole of the universe and set us free, as all rebel writing can. It can always make you bolder.

We constantly underestimate the power of words in our personal lives. Words bond us, one to the other. I am closer to my friend and more respectful of his thoughts since he shoved that soggy note with its smeared blue ink in my hand. I would have never wanted to miss that moment.

Just as we take words for granted, we take each other and our precious moments together for granted. We live ordinary lives, when what are truly available to us are the Extraordinary Lives of magical contrast and the strong unbreakable fibers of miracles.

So I challenge you to the Extraordinary Life. How brave are you? How can you enfold a life worth living into the grandest of experiences?

Step out of bounds and play life in the most extraordinary way that you can imagine.

Exercise: What would your life look like if you said what you meant and meant what you said? What would your life become if you took on the Extraordinary Life outside the box of limitations? What one thing can you do now, today, to start the process? Is there someone you need to say something to?

Go to the page and write the backbone out of these questions. If you are brave enough, send me a letter or essay telling me about the Extraordinary Life you are discovering and letting unfold from your pages.

Stress Less Teens

If you think teens are not
shaping our future, that their words and actions don't seriously
mean much in the big picture,
you are asleep
at the wheel
and you are doomed to crash
unless you wake the hell up
and put on the brake
Now!
Lee Travathan, taken from a speech before an international
conference of broadcasters.

For three years I helped kids leave gangs and encounter their forbidden dreams by teaching them *Extraordinary Thinking*, *Partswork*, and rebel writing exercises. Some say that about 1,600 kids in three states left, some say more, some say less. Three have been executed for their choices. It is a tough life.

Today is one of the biggest days for baseball in the US, it's All-Star Sunday. I'm gazing at the baseball that sits atop my computer in its protective sealed see-through box, signed by baseball "old timer" Lou Klimchock. Lou came out a few years ago to help me raise money for my kids and offered them emotional support in their new choices. He heard the true stories of their everyday lives and quietly lowered his head. I passed the Kleenex around the room. No one present in the crowded room could hold back the tears or talk when the kids finished. A few minutes later I said to them, "Who's extraordinary?"

They all yelled as loud as I'd ever heard them, "I am!" I needed the tissues sent my way, lots and lots of tissues.

Lou wrote on the baseball that southern name he knows me by and added, "You are a saint! Nice job." and signed it. He gave all the kids Diamond Magazine T-shirts. You would have thought he gave them each a million dollars. He was bigger than life to them and they were teary and speechless.

Every time I hear a bat crack, I think of Lou. And I smile. Unfortunately, I won't make it to a game today… the pages call… but I will always have Lou Klimchock in my heart. He made a difference in the lives of those kids. He helped them dream bigger dreams; he showed them he was human and caring. His appearance there stated that they mattered and they heard it without words.

Few adults spend enough time helping kids, mentoring them, so the kids are often bumbling around trying to find a way to somewhere, something, but they don't know what. It is disappointing, to say the least. And atrocious… if you want to face the truth, but that's another book.

I recently discovered a 15-year-old writer named Jennifer Clark. Jennifer writes for LA Youth newspaper. She is helping other teens learn to de-stress through writing. I am sharing one of her articles and asking that you share it with your teen or other teens you know. These kids crave our support. They do business with stress that we adults never had to face.

Jennifer has dreams for her writing life. She also writes poetry and screenplays.

She and I spoke casually for a long while last night about writing, independent film, dreams, and saying something that matters. There are no barriers between kids and adults when we see each other as respected equals.

While I encouraged Jennifer to write, she encouraged me to speak to kids in high schools and colleges across the country. We got ridiculous and had a lot of laughs as she imitated me… *the Queen of Rebel Writing*, peering down from my lavish hotel room overlooking New York's Central Park as I complain about the service; but she was serious about inspiring kids. Teens seek inspiration and acceptance. They don't see enough inspiring lives to use as models.

I have taken her advice to heart and will work it into my schedule.

Jennifer, you're a jewel!

Workshops for teen writers commence in Los Angeles in September of 1999. If you would like to sponsor a teen or attend please let me know. If you would like a ***Positive Evaluation*** *of your teen's work, call or fax me for details.*

<u>Write Your Frustrations Away</u>

Jennifer Clark

At times I am so stressed. I feel as if my head is going to explode! I go crazy from within and a dazed and confused expression sweeps across my face. I usually take my rigid fingers and creep them through my hair. "You're stressed out!" I'll think to myself.

Tranquility and sincere relaxation is what I need. I'll resort to what soothes me most: free writing. My mind is overtaxed at times, just like everyone else's. Writing just allows me to free myself from what sometimes seems like a mental prison. It helps if I make a list of the emotions I'm feeling at that moment. Then I try to relate them to the stressful incident. It doesn't matter how silly my paragraphs become, just the act of releasing the diverse thoughts in my mind helps me cope.

Several weeks ago, I was under pressure because I was on deadline for writing essays for a summer program. I keep wondering, how will my essays stand out from all the other applicants? I just didn't want my essays to seem boring. But with my mind confused and me feeling chaotic, I had to spend several hours just writing whatever came to mind. It didn't matter how non sequitur the paragraphs became. I recall how I ended up writing about four or five different subjects ranging from school to friends to the weather that day. Just the process of writing released my tension.

After free writing, I was able to write the essays with ease. My mind was clear and the thoughts that I wanted to convey became simple to explain. Free writing is a wonderful way for me to cope with stress.

Personal Notes:

Living
The Extraordinary Life

Life means to have something definite to do – a mission to fulfill – and in the measure in which we avoid setting our life to something, we make it empty. Human life, by its very nature, has to be dedicated to something.

Jose Ortega Y Gasset

This last chapter is delivering on the page. And just like a human child, it has come in its own time and in its own way. I did not know today when I began if it would present itself. How appropriate that the book wrap on All-Star weekend… I do so love to hear the bat crack. I'm about to hit a homerun! Ahhhhh, and there it goes! Sheer heaven. Determined ecstasy.

It is 6PM. In one hour Katherine Borges, a popular Virginia poet and writer from Charlottesville, will call in for our Sunday chat to see how her upcoming book, *Bare Tree*, is going. It is a perfect day here in the Hollywood hills. Yes, life is consequently, intensely, and explicitly benevolent.

Just as I type these words earsplitting thunder has smacked in the sky and torrential buckets of rain are now flooding down on what was just moments ago an absolutely clear sunny day.

Why just now, just as I inscribe these wrap words? It has not rained for eons in LA.

More crashing thunder… and now, magnificent light shows over the Hollywood sign high up on the hill above me. I'll close the windows till it passes. The wind is puffing the huge splats of rain in and sending leaves flying into the courtyard. I am laughing and loving it. The show is altogether torrid and swift as the sky clears its massive lungs out onto the earth carelessly. And now the sky has darkened as the rain comes down in gray-white sheets.

This is my extraordinary life... a life of miracles, odd synchronicities and occurrences.

As the lightening and thunder shriek through the upper atmosphere, I feel peaceful here typing away. In early adulthood I developed affection for the sounds of a good storm. They have unceasingly made me feel safe and alive, sensual and free, like now.

How extremely appropriate. Thanks for the ceremonial exhibition, God.

An actress friend has just rung in on her cell using my priority code, the only thing that could get me to answer the phone just now.

"Sweetheart, did you just finish your book?" she asked in excitement.

"I am just now. It's wrapping as we speak."

"I knew it! God... what a display for you, huh?"

"Yeah. Sweet, as sweet as Big Sweetie, and just as dazzling."

We laughed and I told her I had to push on. We said our I love you's and I went on to make a document copy of the book on Zip drive just in case the power goes while I type.

There will be a week of edits and such and it will all be done casually. I will have my own private celebration with God and then with friends. And I will sleep, yes; I will sleep deeply and often.

As my thoughts begin to settle the rain softens and the thunder becomes expediently subtle, not a bellow but a moan. The lightening is kind-hearted and calming and the rain is tender to the plants hit so hard just moments ago. God and I are dancing. Loving each other... snuggling and smiling.

I made a book, a living thing, a child, a guide, and a healer - maybe a mess in the eyes of strenuous critics. I have made a very good thing. The universe has come forward to celebrate.

There will be a second book that goes deeper into the spiritual aspects of rebel writing and chatting with God, but in closing the birth of this one, I wish you to take these kind thoughts to heart.

You are not now, nor have you ever been, ordinary. You are an extraordinary being possessed of and possessing great wisdom and delicate tenderness. Like a square peg in a round hole, you were not meant to fit into an ordinary world.

Your beauty is rapturous and your spirit is indefinable, it is miraculous beyond imagination.

The mysteries of life are to be lived, savored, and cherished, like the sudden fit of grandeur as I wrap this book.

The world is *yours*… and so is the page. The page will grant you all that it has to offer and all that you are amenable to take possession of.

All of this means nothing if you do not love. So, I say to you now that I have gifted you this book out of my love for you. I don't need to know you; this love is vast and spiritual. It is not about who you are; it is about *what* you are, a spiritual being maintaining a human experience. Joint tenants of this earth, perhaps at one time a physical brother or sister, father or mother, friend or lover. But always a spirit sibling of the same creator living the same dream… *us.*

We are the truth. We are the mystery. We are the image. We are precious beyond words.

Are some of the concepts in this book unnatural? To the common mind… oh yeah, sure. But, what the hey, they work. Do what works. Always do what works. And then do more of it.

I thank you for being willing to ponder the extraordinary life, the writer's life, and a fresh thoroughfare. It is a wondrous thing to think that you have either purchased or been gifted my book that wrote itself *out* from the page. There literally isn't a word to describe my gratitude.

Your life is phenomenal. If you don't think it is maybe you have not looked into it earnestly enough. Maybe it is time to discover your Extraordinary Life hidden in the page. Maybe it is time to discover you… the *extraordinary you* on and off the page.

Bless you.

Write anywhere.
Write everywhere.
Write everything.

~ Love Note ~

As this book was being put to bed, America lost a favorite son. May we remember that he is still with us and that his was a life well lived.

In memory of John F. Kennedy Jr., whose rebel spirit graced the pages of George Magazine.
He was one of us.

Author Info

I would love to hear your thoughts on this book, how it has helped you and what your friends think and feel about it. Info on my web site and other such details can be found here. Workshop schedules, evaluation fees, consultation info and upcoming project news is located on the site. May you rebel write for all the days of your wonderful life, and in each moment so precious, I pray my gift has made your life experience and journey a touch more valuable to you.

Ms. Lee Travathan

Awesome Presence Productions
Hollywood
323-957-0358
Fax: 323-957-0059

E-mail: leetravathan@earthlink.net
Web site: www.hollywoodrebelwriter.com

About the Author

Lee Travathan is a writer and independent film maker living and working in Hollywood, California. She writes about her extraordinary relationship with the page and with the town she loves so deeply. She explodes the common mythology around writing that tends to make it difficult for most. When people take her workshops on Rebel Writing or read her work, they discover a new world hidden in the page and begin to write almost immediately.

Her new book, *Rebel Writer,* wrote itself out of the page in twenty days, and gives a full view of how that was done. The end of 1999 will complete her next book, *Rebel Writer Two,* and her feature film, *Journals,* will begin shooting in early winter.

Ms. Travathan can be reached via e-mail: leetravathan@earthlink.net

9 781585 003976